Sally Bayley is a Teaching and Research Fellow at the Rothermere American Institute, University of Oxford and a Lecturer in English at Lady Margaret Hall, Oxford. She has written widely on visual responses to literature, including a jointly-authored study of Sylvia Plath's relationship to the visual arts: *Eye Rhymes: Sylvia Plath's Art of the Visual* (Oxford University Press, 2007) and co-edited a collection of essays of Plath as a cultural icon, *Representing Sylvia Plath* (Cambridge University Press, 2011).

In 2010 she published a study of Emily Dickinson as a way of thinking about America's relationship to space and place. *Home on the Horizon: America's Search for Space, from Emily Dickinson to Bob Dylan* (Peter Lang, 2011) explores evolving American ideas of home, with Dickinson at its centre.

Sally is now completing a literary memoir about growing up in an all-female charismatic household and her escape by reading.

The Private Life of the Diary

THE
PRIVATE LIFE
OF
THE DIARY:

From Pepys to Tweets

SALLY BAYLEY

unbound

This edition first published in 2016

UNBOUND
6TH FLOOR MUTUAL HOUSE
70 CONDUIT STREET LONDON WIS 2GF
WWW.UNBOUND.CO.UK

© Sally Bayley, 2016

While every effort has been made to trace the owners of copyright material reproduced herein, the publisher would like to apologise for any omissions and will be pleased to incorporate missing acknowledgments in any further editions.

Typesetting by Bracketpress

A CIP record for this book is available from the British Library

ISBN 978-1-78352-222-4 (trade hbk)
ISBN 978-1-78352-223-1 (ebook)
ISBN 978-1-78352-261-3 (limited edition)

Printed in Great Britain by Clays Ltd, St Ives Plc

1 3 5 7 9 8 6 4 2

For Talia: may you always be becoming.

Dear Reader,

The book you are holding came about in a rather different way to most others. It was funded directly by readers through a new website: Unbound. Unbound is the creation of three writers. We started the company because we believed there had to be a better deal for both writers and readers. On the Unbound website, authors share the ideas for the books they want to write directly with readers. If enough of you support the book by pledging for it in advance, we produce a beautifully bound special subscribers' edition and distribute a regular edition and e-book wherever books are sold, in shops and online.

This new way of publishing is actually a very old idea (Samuel Johnson funded his dictionary this way). We're just using the internet to build each writer a network of patrons. Here, at the back of this book, you'll find the names of all the people who made it happen.

Publishing in this way means readers are no longer just passive consumers of the books they buy, and authors are free to write the books they really want. They get a much fairer return too – half the profits their books generate, rather than a tiny percentage of the cover price.

If you're not yet a subscriber, we hope that you'll want to join our publishing revolution and have your name listed in one of our books in the future. To get you started, here is a £5 discount on your first pledge. Just visit unbound.com, make your pledge and type **privatelife** in the promo code box when you check out.

Thank you for your support,

Dan, Justin and John
Founders, Unbound

MY FIRST DIARY

When I was seven years old my mother sent me abroad, alone. I carried one small canvas bag containing a camera and a diary-notebook. My instructions were clear: 'Take as many pictures as you can and write down everything you see. Switzerland is a very beautiful country and you'll see lots of important things. Don't waste it on rubbish. If you run out of pages, buy another notebook. Don't skimp, and keep your handwriting nice.'

My mother's brief was this: I was being sent to Switzerland as a reporter, a documentarian. My adventure, like my diary, was not my own. I was to bring all the big events, the sights and the sounds, back home and share them among those who were less fortunate than myself. As Pooh Bear might say, it would contain <u>Very Important Things</u>.

From the first, my diary was never private: it belonged to my mother, my aunt, my grandmother, my brothers and cousins. My diary was already public, already owned. It was never my friend. I could tell it nothing awkward, embarrassing, shameful or pathetic. I could not be homesick or lonely or afraid or bored. My diary forced me to be brave and heroic, to muster more of the grown-up than I could manage. It asked me to be extraordinary.

As the aeroplane lurched out of Gatwick, I pulled the new diary from my bag. My aunt had chosen it, as she had chosen my penpal and my host. Its purple satin cover was intimidating, too special and occasional. What could I possibly experience that would deserve such a thing? How could I really write anything in it? I had to edit out anything that would 'let me down' as my mother would say. 'Don't let yourself down, Sally. Make an effort.' But surely a real diary doesn't ask its keeper to make an effort? Isn't the whole point of a diary that it does allow you to let yourself down; to let go of the coherent and intact story, the picture-postcard version of events? My seven-year-old self wanted to scribble in it; to draw pictures of the funny people on the plane; to cry over it when I felt homesick and lonely, as I often did over the next few weeks; to paste in all the chocolate wrappers from all the chocolate bars I was given by kind Swiss aunts and uncles; to draw rude pictures of people sounding too French. None of this was going to be very satisfactory for the family album or the Show-and-Tell session at school.

Over the course of four weeks I tried to impress my diary. I saved up lots of big words and big sights and I wrote them down. I tried to make everything sound like an Asterix adventure. Every day was filled with difficult and foreign things but I managed all of them: the Gauls, the Britons, the Romans and the Swiss. I took them all on. I ate rabbit and duck and lots of smelly cheese. I spoke my well-rehearsed French phrases and wrote down new ones. I shook everyone's hand. I made friends with a boy called Michel in the village fromagerie. I kissed him. I watched his parents chop cheese and sausages. I watched my hosts make raclettes and fondue and homemade pasta. I even tried reading *Daisy Miller* in French and I wrote that down (a lie; I read it in English). I recorded a few conversations and then checked my French spelling, which took several nights with a dictionary and lots of crossing-out. Who was I trying to impress and was it working? When I went to Berne I took lots of photographs of the bears but most of them were smudgy and misty. So I tried to draw the bears and describe them but I couldn't draw and my Berol pen kept running out and I was too tired to ask for another one (in French). I became anxious. I had promised my mother I would write up every day and this day of all days had been <u>A Very Important Day</u>. I mustn't let it slip away. Today had been <u>Berne</u>, the Swiss capital. Today had been <u>The Berne Bears.</u>

But what happened in between all this perfectly edifying experience? Where did the real experience go, the off-the-record moments when my diary-self was shut off and I was just a lost child in a Swiss village staying with a family she barely knew? I remember wandering around in a large garden full of knotted trees feeling like Mary Lennox from *The Secret Garden*. Where was the lonely and scared seven-year-old girl? The girl who knew how to ask for the loo and for directions to the bus station but could never say that she was too tired to stay up another hour and listen to boring adults talk about 'Madame Peterman' and her house at the top of the hill.

The diary I brought home from Switzerland held none of the things I remember now: eating too much chocolate under the bedcovers at night; the terrible anxiety that I might die from eating a shot rabbit; the shame of being sick over a croissant after a long car journey uphill (mountains). And the crushing loneliness of being alone all the time with adults speaking French. There was nowhere to be myself, not even in my diary. Perhaps this was what it was like to be an adult: in the adult world everything was about making an effort: about 's'il vous plaît' and 'merci'. Where was the diary I dreamed of, my best friend and confidante; the soft beautiful thing I slipped under my pillow at night?

*

My attempts at keeping a diary were inauthentic: a bad performance in being adult. I had missed the point: personal diaries don't ask us to be good grown-ups. Our diary is the ideal boyfriend, girlfriend or best friend, someone who won't abandon us, however bad our tantrums and misbehaviour. Even Greg Heffley, the touchy teenager of Jeff Kinney's *Diary of a Wimpy Kid*, reluctantly admits to dumping his real feelings in his diary or 'journal' as he insists on calling it (N.B.: diaries are for sissies).[1] True diaries contain overspill; they batten down thoughts and feelings for which, in the everyday world, there is little time and space. Diaries can bare souls and anchor lives. Emotionally speaking, they pick up the straying and splintering pieces of ourselves, those moods, atmospheres and secrets that might otherwise ruin situations and relationships. We can say to a diary what we wouldn't dare say to anyone else. Diarising is free therapy, a place where we can project all the mess and maelstrom of our unresolved, teenage identities.

A diary is a form of identity-practice and self-production, a workshop for our future selves. Despite what they might say, most diarists believe, as they write, in a future. But diaries are also proficient escape artists, Houdinis of the present moment, and while they may diligently try to document and reflect upon the day, they are always and inevitably behind the times, always just a little bit belated. The life led and the life recorded are not the same thing and as such, diaries are radically selected and edited biographies; they are lives with many missing parts. This book will tell the story of the diary as a biography; the story of the diarist as they move through the stumbling plot of life.

We might think of diaries as failed coming of age novels, or such novels in parts. Certainly they are uneven and subjective narratives, often repetitive and interrupted. Sometimes they fail to conclude. But at their best they can offer brilliant shards of glistening, extravagant, entertaining, inimitable, unrepeatable insight. A diary entry is as long or as brief, as rich and as interesting as the whim and interest of its writer for its subject, which brings us back to life. When we read a diary we are assessing the quality and value of a life led. Diaries invite us to judge and criticise, to sneer and snigger, to giggle and to gasp. The diarists in this book are as absorbing as the moments they relate, which is the peculiar pathos of the diary-form. Within a diary the lived moment is tantalisingly close, so near and yet so far, just around the corner, just over the page, just over there, spied in a glimpse or a glimmer. Then gone.

A diary can make for bitterly nostalgic reading. Diaries can bring uncomfortable speculations, wishful thinking, sorrow and regret. 'What if' is the diary's inevitable temporal mode. What if I had, what if I hadn't, what if I were, what if I weren't? The diarist who reads back his own diary after a lapse of time can never escape the 'what if' situation. Inexorably, diaries ask their keepers to dwell, as Emily Dickinson hinted, on the possibility of alteration and self-revision, of magical thinking. The unspoken philosophy of the diary is a terrifying philosophy of change.

Virginia Woolf and Samuel Pepys

For the young Virginia Stephen (later Virginia Woolf), a diary was somewhere she could extract the day's most difficult and irritating happenings.[2] Her diary helped sort and smooth the day's sharp edges, which, as a child, are often constituted by other people's plans. Woolf's early entries are full of the disturbances made by other people, a comic-book sequence of silly social arrangements:

> *Sunday 7 February*
> Got up about half past 10. Adrian and Nessa and I went out into the gardens, and so did Stella and Jack, but separately – The ice on the pond all thawed, and boats sailing – The dogs have all got their muzzles off by this time … Nessa waved her umbrella wildly and screamed at Shag and the spotted one, till they slunk away in dismay. Eustace Hill and Scamp for luncheon. After lunch, Mrs. Kay and her two little Kays came, and the two little Kays examined the bugs they are going to collect. Finished the 3rd vol of Scott, and began the fourth, and finished at last Queen Elizabeth – Now the question is what shall become of her – She is far too beautiful to lie about the nursery at the mercy of the ink pot or Pauline, and far too big to live in any of our bookshelves. Bognor settled on for tomorrow. Two vols. of Scott and the Newcomes shall go with me.[3]

Barely fifteen, Virginia Stephen knows only too well that adult society is harried, hurried and reliably absurd. Family life is a mess and a muddle. Nothing or no one is peaceful. Hallways and doorways are full of bodies and loud voices. Doors are opening and closing. Greetings and farewells are constant and draining. There are too many smiles and tears.

The only option is to go outside, but even outside nothing is very seemly. Gestures are exaggerated and overdone. Umbrellas are as wild as excitable dogs. Dogs, people and objects all merge. It doesn't really matter where we are – inside or outside – because nothing is still or calm. People are coming and going, conversations and plans are interrupted, the day is all at sea.

Having grown up in a house full of people, I recognise the choreography of chaos that is daily family life. Hallways and doorways are permanently stuffed with people and their belongings: wellies, anoraks, bikes, buckets and spades, prams and babywear. There are always obstructions and interruptions. Moments are precarious and invasions are imminent. Space is never yours and there is never enough. As my mother liked to put it of 'us lot' (twelve children, of whom four were hers), 'There's never a moment's peace with you lot hanging about … pests, that's what you are … pests! For God's sake go and play outside!' For my mother, who hated bugs and insects – they ruined her beloved roses – her children were just something else she'd prefer to spray away.

Diaries plunge us into the whirlpool of other people's lives. Before long we are up to our reading-waist in it, whatever 'it' is. Reading Woolf's early diary, I sense that something seismic is going on in her family life. Emotion is charged, feelings are fraught, familial patterns are suddenly shifting. A young man has stepped across the threshold; an engagement has just been announced. Virginia's beloved half-sister, Stella Duckworth, has recently become betrothed to Jack Hills. Soon twenty-six-year-old Stella will disappear into a new life and Virginia's only remaining maternal presence will be as good as dead and gone.

Stella's marriage is a threat to the old way of family life. Categories of existence are no longer so neat. Where does Virginia fit without Stella? This is a moment of painful revision. So far knowledge and experience have been built upon sets and lists: of people (and their dogs), books and places. Virginia clings to her categories as a mainstay. Her diary helps her with that.

*

Categories and lists are a means of dealing with the precarious shifts and movements in adult life. One way of dealing with this family schism is to begin to record people separately; to remember in what order they left the house for Hyde Park pond; to draw up a list of moving parts, then carefully parse them into phrases. To remember who you love better and best; to turn your diary into a geometry of affection.

Who you are in relation to others is important for understanding your place in the world. 'Adrian, Nessa and I' now move about separately from 'Jack and Stella'. New sets have formed. When she writes, 'Now the question is what shall become of her', teenage Virginia is not only speaking of her cherished biography of Queen Elizabeth. She also means Stella. Stella is her far too beautiful volume, her most precious lived chapter, her motherly monarch. 'Now' is also the beginning of losing Stella: Stella is still there but Stella, in some sense, has already gone.

Diaries are discreet managers of gaps and intervals in thinking and feeling, where thinking and feeling become too painful. The most unorthodox of narrators, our diary voice permits all sorts of breakdowns in method of being, all kinds of inconsistency and irrelevancy, all manner of distraction method and technique. 'Now' is the extended moment that is Stella gone for ever. Now is the beginning of mourning.

Yet there is something beyond the silly and hysterical parts of Virginia's social world, something more steady and civil than the arrival of bothersome people with pesky-sounding dogs: Virginia's beloved books, her constantly circulating library, her easy traffic with books. Her list of books ends most days. Books seal off her world and comfort her mind. It is more important to consider where she might store her large history of Queen Elizabeth than to think too much about the dreaded trip to Bognor. Bognor is more Stella and Jack; Bognor is betrayal.

For fifteen-year-old Virginia Stephen, diary writing is a form of note-taking during a period of painful familial flux. Observations are geared towards social adjustments and new arrangements. But beneath the social recording there is a very serious cataloguing of books read and raced through, books offering a solid bedrock of words, books bringing calm. Her diary is a place for recording her massive mental advance by reading, her conquistador-style raid on the history of England through George Babington Macaulay, Rome through Livy and the French Revolution through Thomas Carlyle. Reading and recording social history can help her face the familial flux. Tucked at the bottom of her diary entries is her private archive, her deepest storeroom, her library-museum, her ever expanding set of shelves, her future, secret self.

After Bognor – filled mainly with wind and rain and difficult bicycle rides – Virginia and her brothers and sisters return to their house at Hyde Park Gate. Among a general atmosphere of gloom, preparations for Stella's wedding begin. Losing Stella is another form of losing her mother, her mother who died two years before. Losing Stella and beginning her first (surviving) diary are closely related. Stella, in a sense, is Woolf's first diary, Stella and her sister Nessa. Entry after entry begins with a roll call of her sisters' names, reminders of the structure of her affections, the source of her deepest feelings: 'Nessa went to drawing in the morning. Stella and I meant to go to High St. but she insisted upon putting the books in the nursery tidy, so that it was too late to do anything, but bicycle once or twice up and down the road.'⁴ As much as you might love them, sisters take up your time. They boss you about. Sisters have their own ideas and plans. Who and where you are in the sibling line determines who you will be later in life. Virginia's diary reminds her of this. Nessa always sounds far more important because she is always going 'to drawing'. Nessa is also drawing herself away.

For much of her life Virginia Woolf will be a mourner of lost sisters, sisters who once arranged her, sisters she arranged herself around. Later there will also be lost brothers. But for now, and perhaps for ever, she will be enthralled to the idea of Stella and Nessa, her sisterly sweethearts, her first diary loves.

*

Then, in the midst of all this packing and compressing of lives, arrives Samuel Pepys, great naval administrator and diarist, talented overseer of chaos.

Pepys is Virginia's appointed household god and historical intercessor. He is her 'dear Pepys'. Among the turmoil of Stella leaving, we learn that Virginia has been taking comfort in reading the diaries of Samuel Pepys, all six volumes. Pepys is her diary hero and role model, another father figure who slips in from the calm recesses of her reading life. It seems appropriate that the chronicler of the most seismic shift in English history – the reinstatement of Charles II following the traumatic events of the interregnum period and the execution of Charles I – should preside over this shaky moment in family history. Dear Pepys, she tells herself, will be 'the only calm thing in the house'.[5]

Pepys arrives at the end of a family era. On Friday, April 2nd 1897, Virginia Stephen tells her diary: 'This is the last Sunday of Stella Duckworth.' The sentence reads like an execution. Next week Stella will be part of the entourage of 'Mr and Mrs Hills' waiting to cross France for their honeymoon. The house is in chaos, the 'drawing rooms are still topsy turvey and will not recover'. It is 'the beginning of the end', the end of the precocious child, Virginia Stephen, and the beginning of the future novelist, essayist, critic, playwright, diarist, letter-writer, wife, friend, lover and sister still, Virginia Woolf.[6]

*

Diaries are repositories for moments often missed in the humdrum routine of daily life. They tell small stories unheard and unspoken. They keep secrets. They tell separate, hidden histories. But all stories need good tellers, and, together, Woolf and Pepys might be considered the ideal godparents of the diary's story and its long, historical habit. Taken together, the diaries of Woolf and Pepys seem to do everything: order space and time; collect information; reflect upon history both near and far; join the gaps between the life lived and the life upon reflection. But more than this, Woolf and Pepys include us in conversation; they are, above all, good conversationalists. They talk as generously to us, their snooping readers, as they talk to themselves. We read their diaries because they seem to invite us in; because so much of what their diaries cover is the petty and the personal as much as the larger picture. We feel human in their company and so we are grateful, relieved.

Diaries need not always be grand. On the contrary, they allow us to stoop quite low. The diaries of Samuel Pepys and Virginia Woolf are littered with complaints – snipes and jabs at servants, lovers, husbands and wives, domestic arrangements, the small and petty details of daily circumstances, the bother of life. At the same time their diaries offer generous historic panoramas, they pay attention to grander schemes. In Pepys's case this is the Dutch wars of the 1660s and the Great Plague; in the case of Woolf it is two world wars, one of which she lived through and the other whose looming terror she recorded until days before her death. In their doting commitment to the precarious art of diary writing, Woolf and Pepys are this book's heroes.

*

Diaries and journals are a means of becoming, an aid in growing up or growing older. Diaries also assist in our favourite patterns of regression. In the company of Pepys (the fourth volume already), young Woolf admits to going to bed 'very furious and tantrumical'.[7] Her days are not going as she would wish, and so she supplements them with a furious amount of historical reading. Pepys is part of this, for Pepys reminds her of the longevity of the diary's promise, its confident, rather bolshie handling of history. Pepys takes her away from the petty dilemmas of what going-away dress would best suit

Stella; what colour of bridesmaid's dress she should wear. Woolf tells us that 'it is a miracle that I escape to write this.' But escape she does, consistently and persistently. What inspires the miracle – the daily commitment to recording herself in time – is Pepys: 'Gave back Sterling and got Pepys diary.' It is Monday, March 29th 1897.[8] Already she has managed three full months of her diary life. She has another fifty to go. Pepys spurs her on.

Spending Your Personal Time

Historically speaking, diaries emerge from a system of account-keeping: the public world of work and production. In the fourteenth century Florentine merchants kept 'family books' or 'libri di famiglia', as extensions of their household accounts. The roots of the modern-day diary emerge from this practice.[10] The father of the diary, Samuel Pepys, was a good diarist perhaps because his professional life asked him to be a good accountant. As the navy's leading administrator and keeper of its books, diary writing was but a step away. We will never know exactly why Pepys began to keep a diary, but certainly there must have been some sense of wanting to say something about the tumult of contemporary events – the dramatic restoration of Charles II – as well as an urge to reflect upon his own life. Political history was urgently felt and Pepys wrote himself, quite literally, into the documentary scheme of things.

Whatever the case, on January 1st 1660 he began writing in a brown calf-bound notebook, a cut above the common memorandum book. Pepys framed its pages with red ink, ruling margins along the top and outer limits of the pages: seven inches down, five inches across. Supplementing the diary with separate sheets of paper or what he later called a 'by-book', Pepys often made notes on his diary entries before writing them up.[11] We might think of this as a form of preparation before the final composition, before he poured the substance of his day into that red-ruled frame.[11]

As Pepys demonstrates so well, the modern diary emerges from a mentality of expenditure, a system of daily account-keeping in which time and the unit of the day are the chief resource. Suddenly a day could mean something not only chronologically but also fiscally. A day became a unit of time worth noting but also worth spending well.[12] Pepys's visit to John Cade's Cornhill stationers in December 1659 marked the beginning of a new relationship with dailiness.

In its crudest form, the diary is a series of dated record-ings.[13] Dates hover over the beginning of any entry, anticipat-ing stories and events, something worth recording. To a great extent, a diary entry is not complete unless christened by a date. Samuel Pepys and Virginia Woolf, central characters in this book's story, both dutifully dated their entries. Diaries begin with thinking about the time and date, the place and space of a moment, an event; the modern-day date diary or personal organiser is simply an extension of the eighteenth-century almanac. By 1792 America's *The Old Farmer's Almanac* was selling as well as the Bible. Designed to fit inside a pocket, the almanac was the eighteenth-century equivalent of the iPhone or Filofax.[14] With the arrival of the modern calendar, the day was secured as the conventional unit of lived time. The diary privileges personal moments. Take London's Plague year of 1665: Pepys turns the year into his moment. Reading Pepys that year we are comforted by the extraordinary difference between his circumstances and those of his fellow citizens. But diaries privilege difference. They produce individual strands of life – or 'ligatures' as Woolf put it – which tie themselves into unique formations.[15] Diaries produce inimitable cycles of life such that one year can never be read like another. They are begun in the belief that life is a unique and interesting business.

*

In the late sixties, John Lennon submitted a 'diary for the future' to Aspen, the self-styled 'multimedia magazine in a box'. It began like this:

January 1 Wednesday, 1969
Got up – went to work – came home
Watched telly – went to bed.

January 2 Thursday, 1969
Got up – went to work – came home
Watched telly – went to bed.
   'The Lennon Diary 1969'[16]

A facsimile of a pocket diary, Lennon's contribution was designed to be a projection of the following year. Almost every entry was filled with the same banal report: 'Got up – went to work – came home – Watched telly – went to bed.' The only relief to this tedious litany comes with a holiday entry on July 14th: 'Went to Majorca', followed by a series of blank days and then, on July 26th, the cheeky, 'Came back'.

Lennon's arty attack on the diary is also an attack on the humble unit of the day, steeped as it is (for most of us) in ordinariness. The diary, after all, celebrates ordinariness and embraces wholeheartedly what Lennon's former band mate Paul McCartney lyricised as 'just another day'. So why bother recording it? Why trespass upon someone's private life, even if he is John Lennon, with the presumption that we will find something interesting? In Lennon's pop-art world the unit of the day has become so dispensable, so fashionably wasteful as to be completely blank. The future is nothing more than a mechanical repetition of the past. Life has no mystery and days can never be anything special or sacred.

As Daniel Defoe's most deprived of diarists Robinson Crusoe reminds us, counting days is a rather desperate form of survival; certainly it is not living, but, rather, getting by. In the twenty-first century our sense of time is at once so precious and debased, so far removed from the sacred liturgical order of the day divided into prayers – the medieval tradition of the Book of Hours – that one day is pretty much like any other. Today, diary-keeping is an endangered species of experience; the time and space for the diary's reflective art has been lost in our compulsion to dash through our hours and days.

Some of us still keep pocket diaries – the equivalent of a pocket watch or egg-timer – as a means of keeping ourselves in temporal check. But since the late nineties pocket diaries have gradually turned digital, from the BlackBerry or Palm operating systems – once reserved for the smart corporate business man or woman – to the now almost socially ubiquitous smartphone.[17] These days, from my iPhone or iPad I can keep track of my future movements and obligations through slick digitalised calendar and diary functions.[18] I can also, if I wish, upload 'Chronicle' to my iPad or iPhone, a journaling app that allows me to paste images alongside my typed text. If I use PhatPad, an app suitable for iPhones, I can generate, by means of a stylus, the feel and effect of handwriting.[19] In 2015 the intimate world of paper has all but disappeared. Only a few of us cling to the old-fashioned notebook or journal in which to write our thoughts. I do so mainly as a form of indulgent nostalgia for the child I once was, flitting about the world with a pretty notebook and Berol pen, a butterfly with paper. I write on paper in order to feel something more visceral, more real. I remember the weight of paper on bare skin as I sat, perched, at the end of the pier looking out to sea, paper crinkled at the edges from a salt wind.

At the university where I teach, I see my students reverting, particularly during exam time, to the comfort of rainbow-coloured pens, ornate journals and notebooks. Paper is human, and something like skin; it is reminiscent of schooldays and childhood and earlier forms of learning. Writing inside their A4-sized notepads my students take comfort from close contact with paper and pen, the structure of carefully ruled lines. They carry notebooks around like close companions and friends; theirs is a private world of words placed in the right place at the right time. There is something magical in their thinking.

But how much of this culture of tight temporal organisation is dedicated to actual thinking? If we were to ask John Lennon, he'd probably say that few of us are in the business of thinking because none of us has anything much to say; we can leave the saying to pop stars. But then Lennon is making fun of our sense of self-appointment: none of us is doing anything particularly important, certainly nothing sacred. What we are doing is watching time shuttle by. A diary then is also a form of elegy. Anticipating its blank pages, we mourn for what we have just had, what we will never have again.

Diary Life Cycles

At the heart of this book is the delicate membrane between public and private life, a place requiring subtlety and discretion where even in a mature stage of life, and with wisdom on your side, one can falter and fall. This is the place of the diary's spine, the thin vertebrae holding together, but also separating, the joints of public and private life. In public, one cannot afford to fantasise or fictionalise. To do so is to grant your adversaries too many words to play with. Other stories might be written: false ones. Pepys understood this and tucked his diary safely away, encoded in Shelton shorthand, on the dusty shelves of his library.

Diaries embody life cycles. For Pepys, the day is a comforting cycle of routine events, a familiar genus of experience. His day typically begins, 'To my office', 'Up and to my office', 'This morning I was sent for', 'To the coffee club', 'This morning', 'This noon', 'Up early' and ends more often than not with, 'And so to bed'. In Pepys's 'Up and to' there is the sound of swift and efficient action, a body marshaling itself through a fastidious routine. Pepys moves through his day with rigour, so that when the mischief comes, when the cycle goes off course, we relish it. Pepys waking to the sound of the rain at 3am, Pepys startled by the loud mewing of his cat locked in the chamber, his cat leaping upon his bed, are delightful and picaresque disruptions. Suddenly, the day is more 3D.[20] Unexpectedly, we are in the intimate middle of real life.

Virginia Woolf lived and moved through her diary from adolescence to maturity, and though she did not die old, her diary did grow up. As a sort of living organism, it is a textual relative of the green caterpillar lying snug and hidden in the hollow on the Sussex Downs Woolf writes of in her Asheham house diary soon after she is married. Over the course of the days, the caterpillar becomes a chrysalis. A careful and patient entomologist, Woolf watches its slow daily transformation. Not everything she sees is pretty. Metamorphosis, in this case, is a truly 'horrid sight': a monstrous 'snake in movement' with its 'head turning from side to side'.[21] Life as it is born is often grotesque, immobile and helpless. It changes colour, acquires spots. For a moment, perhaps longer, it seems quite monstrous. Woolf's caterpillar is insect life transforming itself, a species coming into a coherent form of being, moving through the peculiar phases of its life cycle.

Woolf's diary enacts a similar process: eventually, by the end of its cycle, an entire life will have spun out through its pages. A coherent species of living and being will have been produced. All the fluttering paper and nervous movements of the hands, the quick scribbling, the peculiar elegance of the handwriting, will produce inky spots and markings of peculiar rarity. Nothing quite like it will have been seen before. Here is a unique record of life as it was lived, with enough speed, carelessness, gaps and exaggeration to feel real.

Diaries, like life, go through stages. This book traces those stages of life as they move and spin, often fleetingly, and with some flutter and trepidation, from chrysalis to butterfly, from youth to old age. Diaries run back and forth between private and public worlds, reporting on both. This book will do the same. Loosely speaking, the first part deals with the diary as a private entity: what Woolf called, in relation to Pepys, her 'secret companion'.[22] The second will focus on the diary as it reports on the public world: Pepys in the hurly-burly world of naval administration and royal affairs, Woolf commenting on the horrifying advance of Hitler.

Diaries establish an identity. They can help us find a place in the world. A diary can provide space for contemplation of the wider world through exploration of nature and through travel. I start by looking at youthful and confessional diarists, such as Sylvia Plath, Susan Sontag and the young Ralph Waldo Emerson, who use their diaries as a form of self-creation. I then turn to diarists writing about time spent in a particular place, home and away, such as Virginia Woolf in her Asheham home in Sussex, and James Boswell in London. Nature brings comfort and a moment of pause; it yields a period of reflection. In natural spaces, the diarist often finds an ideal diary habitat.

But private dalliances cannot last for ever. Diaries rely upon a period of daily solitude which life does not always grant. Events rudely interrupt. In the second, more public part of this book, we encounter diarists entering the public and political world, including America's second President John Adams, British politician Alan Clark and diarists of war such as George Orwell and Evelyn Waugh. Just as public life brings with it all the possibilities of sparkling success and self-promotion, so it also brings all the threat and danger of a rapid fall from grace. In the world of politics and celebrity, scandal is lurking closely around the corner. The final chapter examines what happens when diaries contain dangerous information, the pain and disorder of scandal. Will the diarist survive with his reputation intact, and, if so, who will curate and control how much of his story is told?

By 1668, and at the height of his public success, Pepys is struggling to contain a stressful amount of potential scandal. His affair with his former servant, Deb Willet, has reached a damaging crisis. Elizabeth, his wife, is threatening to tell the world about it, and his days are spent running to and fro between wife and lover. In desperation, he turns to his diary to confess his continuing folly, hoping that the ritual of confession will bring it to an end. But diaries, though they might help us begin projects, cannot stop the ongoing mess and muddle of life.

CHAPTER ONE:

TEENAGE CONFESSIONS

My Diary-Self

As a teenager, I didn't yet know about Cassandra Mortmain, the roaming diarist of Dodie Smith's whimsical novel, *I Capture the Castle*. But I wish I had. I would have wanted to be like her. Most of all I would have wanted to sound like her. I like to think I already did.

> I write this sitting in the kitchen sink. That is, my feet are in it; the rest of me is on the draining board, which I have padded with our dog's blanket and the tea cosy. I can't really say I'm comfortable, and there is the depressing smell of carbolic soap, but this is the only part of the kitchen where there is any daylight left.

Cassandra Mortmain sounds like my fourteen-year-old self. She sounds like someone who knows exactly what she wants. She also sounds as though she knows that she doesn't have it yet, not in the muddled, dirty space where she lives. Cassandra Mortmain is someone who knows how to make the best of a bad lot. She's an improviser of untidy relationships and, unlike me – or rather me, my eight cousins and three brothers in our ramshackle house by the sea – she isn't forced outside. Instead, she camps out in the kitchen sink with her diary-ally.

Cassandra Mortmain keeps a diary because she wants to make some extra room for herself. She's digging a hole through those diary passages, digging down and out of the dilapidated, broken home she finds herself in – a home where the kitchen sink is the only clear space – to a new world. All the space in my house was taken too. And because there was no storage space, except in the dark, damp cellar where we kept our bikes and Mum kept her spring bulbs, everything was always out on show, highly visible, ready to fall over and break. Even in the cellar things sat on the surface, strange names scratched into the mouldy walls, letters surrounded by boxy shapes, letters shut up in prison.

'Nazis,' my aunt said, 'Nazi symbols … the Luftwaffe … they kept prisoners of war down there.' We believed her, because everything my aunt said sounded like God speaking from the clouds. So it must be true.

The cellar was where the Nazis had buried … what? I wasn't quite sure. The men who tried to deliver the coal down the back stairs? My grandmother told me that our house used to have back stairs. Perhaps when the Germans came over on their rowboats at night they found men with dirty black faces creeping about with sacks of coal and they thought maybe these men had murdered some Germans and now they're storing their bodies in our coal-hole.

The coal-hole was our big secret. It was where everything was buried that nobody wanted to think about any more; it was where no one dared look.

*

Writing was the only way I knew of keeping something secret. I had to start carrying a notebook. Women, I noticed, had small notepads and diaries they kept in their handbags and purses; my grandmother had her small pocket-sized red notebook with thick, wide lines where she kept her shopping list; my mother had her posh gold and silver foil-covered date diary, a small book called 'Letts' where she wrote down important dates in her long, thin scrawl that tipped sideways (towards the sea, I always thought, towards the beach, out the front door, across the road, and down to the sea). Mum's handwriting looked like it was always running away. I wanted to copy it and run away too.

So I went to the charity shop on the corner of the Arcade to see if I could find a cheap notebook, something that looked like a diary, but with more room than Mum's small, flat, hard shiny oblong. I wanted something softer; a book with thick pages I could fall into, somewhere I could start to write stories. Oxfam was where Mum went to find new things, things that had been tossed away.

Oxfam was always full of old bicycles and second-hand toys, bashed-up plastic push-along tricycles whose wheels had fallen off and lots of old, scratched records dumped inside squashed cardboard boxes. I turned to the shelves. Everything on the floor was junk. But the shelves held books and cards, things kept in cellophane wrap, things with more prestige. Two shelves up I found a plastic box of cards and notepads, writing paper and exercise books, paper books covered in sunflowers and tulips and daisies, books that wanted to be flower-arrangements. I pulled them down and started to poke through.

'Found what you're looking for?'

The voice behind me didn't sound very pleased. It was the sort of voice that was bound to say next, 'Are your hands nice and clean?'

'I'm looking for a notebook...a diary...something with lines.'

'What sort of diary? Do you mean a diary or a journal? If you mean a journal then you'll have to have a rummage over there. We've got a few old notebooks you could turn into a journal if that's what you mean. Are you trying to practise your handwriting?'

The lady looking at me had a funny smell, the sort of smell that came out of toilets when you were trying to make them smell better. She sounded like Mrs Moose who was in charge of the library at school. Mrs Moose always suspected dirty hands and kept sending us to the toilet.

'The only diaries we have are the ones donated from the Christmas raffle ... they're still nicely wrapped up, so don't pull them open unless you're sure you're going to buy one. They're all about 50 pence or a pound. I hope you have your pocket money with you, young lady?'

Her eyebrows had started wiggling like worms. I thought they might jump off and eat up her face, but before I could keep watching she swished around and walked off, back to the cash register, back to the lady in the pink jumper who was beckoning her to sort out the prices. I turned back to the plastic box and felt through the slippery cellophane. I wanted a book that nobody would bother to pick up if they found it. At the bottom of the pile I found one without plastic. Instead it was covered in a brown paper bag that had been smoothed out along the wrinkles. I touched the surface; it reminded me of the brown paper bags my grandmother brought back from the greengrocers filled with Cox's apples, treats for Mum.

Somebody had covered this book very carefully with brown paper, given it a new skin.

I opened it up and studied the paper. The lines were reassuringly thick and bold, but not too thick I couldn't write over them. They ran delicately off the side of the pages, down the sides, off the edge of the papery cliff.

I took the book to the register. 'I'd like to buy this please. Could you wrap it up?'

The lady with the pink jumper looked at me. 'We don't gift wrap in here. This isn't a gift shop.' She said the word 'gift' harshly, like she was spitting out a pip in an orange.

'I just mean could you wrap it inside another bag so that that bag' – I pointed to the surface of my notebook – 'doesn't get dirty.' I looked back hard at her. 'I'm going to be taking it outside.'

*

'In the journal I do not just express myself more openly than I could do to any person; I create myself,' says American writer, philosopher and aesthete, Susan Sontag, in her published *Early Diaries*, aged sixteen.[23] Sontag's bold statement dispenses with the notion of the diary as a dumping ground for personal stuff. In her diary she will do something rather more formal and serious: she will devise and cast herself; she will play at artist and God.

Of course Sontag's statement is also largely egoistic swagger, something the diary's blank page encourages. Hers is a performance, or rather an audition, in who or what she will become. And so her diary is a place for preening and posturing, for large poses; it is a much-repeated dress rehearsal in selfhood.

5

Unfortunately for her reader, Sontag's juvenile diaries leave little room for irony or self-parody; there are few if any comic subplots. But then she has a loftier intention, to master what the sixteenth-century poet Philip Sidney called 'selfnesse': something close to our contemporary 'self-involvement'. Sontag's only subject is herself, and as such her diaries often turn into a disappointing and tiresome read. Where, we ask, is the intellectual gumption and critical imagination of her essays, the scorn for the ordinary, the snobbish intellect of Sontag, lover of the decadent outsider? Stuck in the middle of Sontag's pimple-ridden narcissism, those of us who read her journals are uncomfortable with what we find there, embarrassed. Should we really be reading this stuff? we wonder. Probably not.

The secondary and more generous reading of 'selfnesse' is 'essence' or 'individuality', even 'personality'.[24] In this latter sense the young Sontag is presenting the essence of what she is in the here and now, a record of her personality as it develops moment to moment. Hers is a live record of her living and growing self; an almost biological, you might even say, hormonal development. If we read her young journal this way we can perhaps redeem her from some of the embarrassment. We might say that in the tradition of the coming-of-age novel, Sontag plots herself; the disappointment for the reader comes with realising that the personal plot of the young Sontag, although intellectually ambitious, is terribly self-involved. But we must remember: Sontag is only sweet sixteen.

Still, Sontag is very knowing about the diary genre and her relationship to it. She realises that any diary writing forces an absurd split between the life led within the diary and the life without. 'There is often a contradiction between the meaning of our actions towards a person and what we say we feel towards that person in a journal,' she confesses.[25] A journal, in other words, encourages the hypocrite in us. It frees us from the necessities of daily life where we regularly swallow our words, bite our tongues and generally try to behave ourselves.

Diaries indulge the weaker parts of our ego. Consequently, our diary persona is often poorly socialised, veering between overly sincere and insincere poses. You wouldn't introduce this personality to your parents. So what does this amount to for the reader? In Sontag's case this often means enduring dramas largely involving her sexual identity, dramas soaked in outbursts of confessional cliché: 'I am almost on the verge of madness ... tottering over an illimitable precipice.'[26] It is hard to take such self-dramatising seriously, and while it might be labelled confessional there is little that is ritualised or sacred.

The Secret Diary of Adrian Mole

Wednesday January 14, 1981.
Joined the library. Got Care of the Skin, Origin of Species, and a book by a woman my mother is always going on about. It is called Pride and Prejudice, by a woman called Jane Austen. I could tell the librarian was impressed. Perhaps she is an intellectual like me. She didn't look at my spot, so perhaps it is getting smaller. About time! ... None of the teachers at school have noticed that I am an intellectual. They will be sorry when I am famous.
  The Secret Diary of Adrian Mole Aged 13 ¾ [27]

Miss Clements read *The Secret Diary of Adrian Mole* to us to finish off the day. That's what she called it; 'finishing off the day'. Mum said it was skiving to read Adrian Mole out loud in class like that (well, she didn't say 'skiving', but that's what she meant).

'What a waste of time ... That isn't literature ... what on earth is she playing at? You're too old for that babyish rubbish.'

My mum spent a lot of time being indignant. But then so did Adrian Mole.

Of course we all understood that Miss Clements was trying to make us feel better about being eleven or twelve, 'the awkward age', my grandmother said. We thought it was terribly grown-up to hear someone talking about their pimples so much, and in any case, Adrian Mole did read books. He was an intellectual. Miss Clements read us Adrian Mole because she wanted to show us that you can have spots and still be clever. You can talk obsessively about your skin and the way you look, but also go to the library and read books. (Now that I think of it that isn't really a very clever thought.) But Miss Clements was sweet and she was trying to make us feel better. She suggested that we all start keeping diaries to help us 'process our feelings'. When I heard that all I could think of was processed sausages and processed cheese, which my grandmother said were 'full of rubbish ... put it straight in the bin!'

We didn't need to show anyone our diary, Miss Clements said. In fact it was better that we didn't. They might be things we want to keep to ourselves, private things, like Adrian Mole telling his diary that he likes this girl called Pandora.

'It's perfectly natural to start liking girls at your age,' said Miss Clements. Michael Roberts started to snigger very loudly when she said that. Miss Clements turned to him and said, 'I realise that speaking about feelings is embarrassing, Michael, but it's all perfectly natural and I want to encourage you to stop feeling bad about your feelings.' Personally, I don't think Michael Roberts felt bad about anything.

When I told Mum about the diary idea she said that Miss Clements was just being 'very silly and self-indulgent'. Mum didn't like the idea of people spending too much time on their feelings. 'The diary of a thirteen-year-old boy is not proper thinking ... it's bound to be full of twaddle [Mum loved the word "twaddle"]. At your age you need something proper to think about.'

Confession

As journal-writers go, Sontag is a direct descendant of the Christian confessional tradition. The history of confession begins in public, with the early Church fathers, whose culture of hierarchical paternalism encouraged clean, shameless public confession. By the time of St Augustine in the fifth century AD, confession had become a form of autobiography, something far more personal. But the sense of a public still lingered. 'To whom am I narrating all this?' asks Augustine.[28] His answer is not God but others: 'that small part of the human race who may chance to come upon these writings'.[29]

Confession arises from a desire to unbury something troubling from the past in order to live more peacefully in the present. It is based on the understanding that someone is listening to our troubles. By the seventh century, the Church had adopted the Celtic monastic practice of spiritual counselling and adapted it to a form of auricular confession in which a priest listened in private to an individual confession of sin. Discretion and privacy were everything, and depended upon the integrity of the individual, namely the priest.[30] After confession, one expects to feel better, whether in church or away from it.

Confession anticipates at least one listener. If we carry that idea into the diary genre, then all diaries anticipate at least one intruder, someone who will try to break in. Sontag is explicit about this: we write journals, she argues, in order to be overheard and found out. We like the idea of someone entering into our holy-of-holies. We even fantasise about it.

But Sontag seems peculiarly amoral in this regard. She remains perfectly untroubled by her decision to violate her lover's privacy by reading their diary: 'Do I feel guilty about reading what was not intended for my eyes? No.' Unabashed, she launches into a social rationale for diary writing, unflinchingly arguing that an essential part of the diary culture is the necessary acceptance of a 'furtive' reader.[32] Naturally, the diary will shock, even harm, the intruding reader. But that is part of its thrill. As Sontag sees it, the diary offers a covert contract between the diarist and their furtive reader, between one lover and another. Each exists in some sense to shock and surprise the other.

At this point I am reminded of Gillian Flynn's expertly vengeful protagonist, Amy Dunne, of the recent bestseller thriller *Gone Girl*. Amy's obsessively planned revenge plot on her husband – a husband she loathes in the most detailed of ways – begins with a crucial false alibi: her diary. Amy's only purpose in keeping a diary is to create a fictional plot that will lay all the blame for her disappearance at the feet of her husband. Coming in the first part of the book, Amy's diary narrative immediately sets up a backstory of a fairy-tale marriage. According to the diary-story, Amy and Nick had been desperately in love until things (Nick) started going wrong. The plot of *Gone Girl* is the cruellest undoing of the American romance story, what Amy in her first diary entry calls the 'Technicolor comic of a teenage girl' falling in love with a boy. As Amy Dunne tells us in this first gushing diary entry, she is a writer and she is in love. She is using this journal to 'get better'. She means as a writer, but in retrospect, after reading on, we realise she is also using her journal to improve her tactics as a saboteur and sociopath. Her journal is an active agent in her malicious gathering of 'details and observations'. She is a brilliant liar, a seductive and persuasive piece of fiction.[32]

Likewise, Sontag's take on the journal is determinedly free of ethics. To her mind, the journal is not a private or personal enterprise; rather it is a social endeavour whose purpose is to extend one individual's knowledge at the expense of another's privacy. Journal-trespass, of the sort Sontag advocates, is a risky business. I might learn something I would rather not. It may hurt. But as Sontag acknowledges, the journal-ego is robust; it 'wins through' to a level of self-confidence that believes, self-righteously, it has something important to say.[33]

*

Born just three months before Sontag, the young poet Sylvia Plath has the same need to show and tell, and like Sontag she wants to sound like God. Plath's journals reveal a young girl craving 'sensation', an ecstatic out-of-body experience that will alter her present state. As a seventeen-year-old, Plath commits to her diary the experience of 'rapture', the overwhelming sensation of her teenage feelings:

November 13, 1949
As of today I have decided to keep a diary again – just a place where I can write my thoughts and opinions when I have a moment. Somehow I have to keep and hold the rapture of being seventeen. Every day is so precious, I feel infinitely sad at the thought of all this time melting farther and farther away from me as I grow older. Now, now is the perfect time of my life.[34]

Plath's 'now' is insistent and self-important. 'Now' is pure feeling and feeling is momentum and change. Later, in her mature poetry, 'now' will turn into a condensed form of dynamic expressionism, the exhilarating alchemy in 'the pure gold baby that melts to a shriek' of her most famous poem, 'Lady Lazarus'.[35] But without the containing force of poetry, without the tight form, feeling is simply a series of self-important assertions that her existence matters. Young Plath craves a perpetual present filled with an intoxicating 'selfnesse'. She wants to drink deeply from her own rich imagination; to lie down in a field of poppies, as Dorothy did, and drift somewhere over the rainbow.

*

We keep journals because we believe they will help us to improve our methods of thinking, generate better choices and finally put an end to all the dithering. By the time she is nineteen, Plath is using her journal in a more practical way: to help her sort through the competing voices in her head. Her choices are stark: either she must sublimate her ego and lead a life in service to others, or she must choose to write, for her own sake. It is a cruel choice and one that splits her down the middle. Before long, her entries start to sound like shouting matches with herself, an effect enhanced by her habit of underlining and capitalisation.[36] Marriage presents itself as a way out of the double bind. And so, with her journal acting as solemn witness, she swears to herself a solemn oath. She will marry: 'I must be clever and obtain as full a measure of security for... So, resolved: I shall proceed to obtain a mate through the customary procedure: namely marriage.'[37]

At nineteen, Plath has already swallowed whole the language and formulas of popular psychology. Within these terms she can only view herself as a neurotic case in need of rescue. What have other women done, she wonders, to free themselves from these terrible choices? She turns to the literary legacy of female neurotics, to her foremother Virginia Woolf: 'Why did Virginia Woolf commit suicide? Or Sara Teasdale – or the other brilliant women – neurotic? Was their writing sublimation (oh horrible word) of deep, basic desires? If only I knew how high I could set my goals, my requirements for life! ... The future?'[38]

This is not confession so much as circular thinking. Plath swims around in anxious circles. This sort of writing squeezes out mental space. It exacerbates her woes. In today's language of popular psychology we might say that Plath's journals reflect a young woman suffering from an anxiety disorder. She is looking to her journal to help her out of this paralysing circle of self-doubt. She must, at some point soon, alight upon an answer. And so she keeps going.

Above all, it is this unwavering belief in her journal speaking back to her that keeps Plath moving through this circle of personal purgatory. Soon she will find her writer's ego, the 'me' that is 'full of rapture'.[39] Soon, she will find her voice. For Plath, as for Sontag, this speaking, feeling 'me' is the writer's ego, something or someone her nineteenth-century journal ancestor Ralph Waldo Emerson conversed with extravagantly and exuberantly.

*

On the brink of the New Year, 1820, sixteen-year-old Ralph Waldo Emerson, with a flourish of rhetorical pomp and circumstance, declared himself a journalist. The future poet and transcendentalist philosopher picked up a notebook and began to write in it. His statement was as serious as any wedding vow or oath: he promised to keep a journal in order to capture the whole of life, the 'wide world' within and without. Emerson blessed his journal world or 'common place book' as he first called it, with a spell. He called upon witches, wizards and fairies to sprinkle the leaves of his book with inspiration: 'O ye witches assist me! Enliven or horrify some midnight lubrication or dream ... to supply this reservoir when other resources fail ... Spirits of Earth, Air, Fire, Water, wherever ye glow, whatsoever you patronise, whoever you inspire, hallow, hallow, this devoted paper – Dedicated & Signed Jan 25, 1820.' [40]

Emerson's is a necromantic journal nativity. His incantation sounds much like Shakespeare's island-bound magician, Prospero, reciting his august spells. While Prospero has an attendant spirit at his beck and call – Ariel, his bearer of magic – Emerson has a journal in which to conjure up a 'brave new world'. His dedication is a piece of magical thinking and a sort of creed. All magicians have props, attendants and magical books. Emerson's journal follows a similar plot. His journal will prop up the life of his mind, his philosophy, his rhetoric and his written word. It will be both workshop and co-worker, and, in the process, will prepare him for his life in the world.

Emerson's journal is a sounding board for his future life. As a student at Harvard University in 1820, he is writing into his future, towards his future self. For this, he needs more space. And so he turns his journal into a grand horizon, his imaginative line between here and there, then and now:

Jan 1820
It is a singular fact that we cannot present to the imagination a longer space than just so much of the world as is bounded by the visible horizon; so that even in the stretching of thought to comprehend the broad path lengthening itself & widening to receive the rolling Universe stern necessity bounds us to a little extent of a few miles only. But what matters it? We can talk & write & think it out.[41]

Emerson's young self demands space, space to stretch out and be. He is an ambitious teenager; he would like, he thinks, before he dies, to enjoy something of infinity. His journal will bridge the gap between the visible and invisible world, between God and himself, between God and his imperious 'me'. He asks, 'Who is he that shall control me? Why may I not act & speak & write & think with entire freedom? What am I to the Universe, or, the Universe, what is it to me?'[42] Emerson's 'me' stands apart from the world. He is in the midst of them, but not of them. His 'me' is special and unique, bursting with the power of personality.

Personality keeps the world apart; it keeps hands off 'me'. When we read Emerson's journals it is impossible to forget personality. It presses down upon us from all sides like a loud and oversized guest in a small room. Listening to the young Emerson we are reminded of a teenage boy shut up in his bedroom posing before his mirror, a boy practising the roles of wizard and superhero, a boy preparing for a testing future.

*

In the world of the diary there is room for divine role-play. For American teen, Sylvia Plath, that space is the 'kingdom' of her bedroom where everything is still pink and princessy. Writing from her room in the summer of 1952, Plath conceives of herself as a monarch installed in a 'kingdom' of fantasy. From her 'throne', she looks down with disdain upon the world beneath her. She scoffs at the middle-class Massachusetts suburbs with their predictable routines of family life and heterosexual hierarchies: father, mother, children, porch, car.[43] Plath's fantasy is a vivid response to memories of herself locked into the menial role of babysitter, months in which 'Liberty' and 'self-integral freedom' perpetually hovered 'around the corner of the calendar'. 'All of life is not lost, merely an eighteenth summer,' she dolefully announces.[44] But, for an ambitious nineteen-year-old, a summer is a long time to waste.

And yet, a summer on, she is still giving children baths and making Devil's Food Cake. Plath is bitterly disappointed. All she can do, she tells herself, is beat a retreat into her dream world. Alongside the dreary piles of washing-up and unfolded clothes will exist this alluring 'dream-bubble'.[45] Her journal will provide an alternative life. There, she will conjure an American dream like no other. In her journal she will conjure her supreme self; she will float free of the depressing thought that she is just another college kid from the Boston suburbs babysitting on her summer break. She may not go as far as Amy Dunne with her sociopathic revenge on domestic life. But instead of Sylvia the au pair, she will call herself the 'Girl who would be God'.[46]

*

Plath's adolescent diaries are a necessary part of her ego development, her egotistical coming-of-age story.[47] At the heart of this story are the thoughts of a girl who longs for omniscience. Plath wants to see everything, and all at once. She wants to be God. But the problem is she doesn't quite know enough. 'I am in the mood for Thundery poetry now. I wish I had the experience to write about it.'[48]

Plath turns to her journal for help in managing the difficult relationship between her internal sense of self and the more compromised reality. What she longs for is to remain steadfast and true to the present moment, the moment of pure sensation, of complete and utter thrill. Her teenage self fears losing contact with that. Her mantra for life is this: 'With me, the present is forever, and forever is always shifting, flowing, melting. This second is life. And when it is gone it is dead … I am the present, but I know I, too, will pass.'[49]

As it happens, Plath's moment has not passed. She now occupies a large place in the popular literary imagination, as a stream of books, articles, films and pieces of fiction continue to memorialise her. Plath continues to live in the present. That she should remain so culturally present seems fitting for a writer who lived so urgently. Plath lived for what she calls 'the burning flash'; that is, intense sensation in the passing word, image, or experience. She powerfully believed that poetic imagery and insight worked transformation, alchemy. Her adult journals open with Joyce's words: 'Hold onto the now, the here, through which all future plunges to the past...'[50]

I confess...

That I didn't read the journals of Sylvia Plath or Virginia Woolf until I was seventeen. I wouldn't have been sophisticated enough to have read them before then. I'd have judged them as harshly and ignorantly as children always do the people who have gone before them, the adults who keep things moving.

To read Plath you have to possess some degree of irony. Much of what she produces is role-play, rhetorical posturing, absurd smoke and mirrors. But irony comes later in life, and sometimes not at all. Her journals have to be read as a personality test: against hers and ours. You can't believe everything she says and she says a lot of the same thing. But then a journal is the right place for banging on. And how, at seventeen or nineteen, was she to know she'd have a peanut-crunching, popcorn-munching worldwide audience?

*

It is easy to condemn Plath for sounding self-involved in her journals, for being what my mother would have called 'selfish'. Being selfish was the worst thing you could be in a house full of women and too many children, a house whose domestic work was done mostly by my grandmother, our indentured labourer and household slave. In my house you were not encouraged to think of yourself. There was no 'I' and 'Me', only

'We'. Everything was a group activity. Nothing was a single choice. How many sausages you ate for dinner was determined by where you came in the genetic line. It was three if you were me, four if you were my older brother, two if you were my younger cousins and brothers, one if you were anyone younger. Nobody knew how many sausages the adults ate because they ate separately from us. There wasn't enough room in our single, multi-purpose room for us all to eat together. In the same room my grandmother did all the washing-up, the laundry and the cooking; it was where we did our homework.

At thirteen I knew nothing of the life or work of Sylvia Plath, whose father died when she was eight leaving her in the care of matriarchs: her mother and her grandmother who cared for her brother and her grandfather, all of them squashed into a small clapboard house in Winthrop, Massachusetts. I knew nothing about Virginia Woolf and her many homes and houses, Virginia Woolf and her many siblings, Virginia Woolf and her one devoted husband. At twelve or thirteen I wouldn't have understood that the reason Virginia Woolf could write so much, the reason we have all those diaries, novels, letters, plays, essays and reviews is because she had a husband and servants. She had what my mum would have called 'Help'. If you're going to be a writer you need 'Help'. 'Help' keeps you from the chronic interruptions of family life that prevent you from plunging (one of Woolf's favourite verbs) into the pool (one of Woolf's preferred images) of mental life. That pool ripples with a limitless present tense. That pool is filled with the 'now' that seventeen-year-old Sylvia Plath summoned into her bedroom. 'Now' is the intensely imaginative present. 'Now' is electric and life-giving.

Housework and shopping don't fit inside that version of the present. Neither do children. Sylvia Plath knew that. As an adult, she struggled to write. With two small children her day was cut into jagged (one of Plath's favourite adjectives) pieces of time, time made up of mealtimes, shopping, cooking, washing, cleaning. It was impossible to write in the day, so she had to get up in the middle of the night. Her writing time was the glassy blue hour as she called it – 4 am – when no one else was awake except the milkman. Thirty-year-old Sylvia Plath wrote to the 'chink, chink' of milk bottles hitting the pavement, the low zoom of the milk cart moving on.

My mother had no idea about this magical 'now'. She'd have scoffed at it. My mother would have thought Virginia Woolf and Sylvia Plath dreadfully selfish for keeping a diary. My mother, who lay in bed for much of my early childhood, didn't have the time or energy to keep a personal diary. She could only manage lists, the names and numbers of people she might need to call upon if things got really sticky (or stickier): the bank manager, the butcher, the greengrocer, our headmaster. She labelled these people 'Accidents and Emergencies'. Now I think of it, they were all men.

CHAPTER TWO

DIARY DAWDLING

Dawdling in Lobs Wood

The first place I went with my new journal was Lobs Wood. I wanted to find a stump of wood to sit on, a chair and a desk outside. Lobs Wood was the place we walked through if we wanted to make ourselves late for school, an island of trees surrounded by cow-parsley, dandelions and stinging nettles and sometimes bluebells. Bluebells came and went. I hadn't worked out that bluebells only came out in late April and early May, depending upon the weather.

But when you're seven, eight, nine, you don't think about months of the year as anything related to natural patterns; flowers are just there or not there. It's the school holidays or it's school; it's the weekend or a weekday. Your sense of time is structured around the school calendar and nothing else. When the holidays come you wonder what on earth you will do to pass the time, because for children or adolescents time is the principal enemy, the perpetual murderer of excitement and interest. There is always too much time to kill. Time, I decided, could be turned into lines in my notebook, my journal, my writing-diary, lines that would lead me away from the present moment into a more daring future. I looked at the chalk-white edges of the book in my hand and I wanted to jump.

*

I don't remember much of what I wrote in my Lobs Wood journal, only the sensation of being outdoors with paper and pen knowing that no one could find me. I was unaccountable to time and space; Robinson Crusoe on his desert island working out what he needs to stay alive. My grandmother had told me that bananas were the perfect food. You could live entirely on bananas for the rest of your life. So I took bananas to the woods and sat on my stump and twisted my pen around my mouth, wondering what to write.

Nobody disturbed me; almost nobody walked through Lobs Wood, except the occasional dog walker. My mum would say that Lobs Wood was the place for dawdling. I think that was mostly what I was doing in Lobs Wood with my journal: I was dawdling, dawdling away the time in between school and home, dawdling away Saturday mornings and afternoons when no one was looking. Dawdling: meaning to move aimlessly, without picking your feet up properly; forgetting what it is you are meant to be doing; stopping off and looking at things instead of hurrying along, playing silly devils. Not going home, not going to school, not doing what any of the adults expect you to do. Dawdling: moving away from the things that trouble you, namely people.

*

Diary writing is a habit requiring time and space, a period of incubation. Virginia Woolf wrote her diary in the 'casual half hours after tea', an interval of time in which she could slip out of her more formal writing-clothes and put on something more comfortable.[51] This was diary-time: an extended 'moment of being' beyond the prim exigencies of the everyday world, where the clock stops and places can suddenly shift. As Woolf knew only too well, her diaries tended to produce writing and thinking of a freer sort. Without a plot or a plan for this slot in the day, her diary might take her anywhere.

In reality, Woolf's diaries mainly moved, as she did, between London and Sussex, but her diarist's imagination was always on the roam. What is most important to the diarist is the immediate time and place of writing things down. Often, this is somewhere away from home, somewhere on holiday. Here, the diarist can enjoy a sojourn, a period of time outside daily life where something extraordinary can be found. Away, abroad, diary life flourishes.

*

In the summer of 1903, twenty-one-year-old Virginia Stephen is preparing to go on holiday to Wiltshire. For seven weeks she will live in the country. She is anticipating a freer life.

Rather than sewing clothes to take with her, she is sewing books to write in, her journal-books. Part of going on holiday is passing through a lot of paper. So she packs paper rather than clothes. 'This is what I mean by getting ready,' she cheerfully announces. 'I collect books on all conceivable subjects & sew together paper books like this I write in.' What excites her is the 'thickness of paper' that will have 'passed through' her mind by the time the holidays are over. Thickness of paper is one way that Virginia measures her distance away from home, the density of her experience. Paper consumption is a form of travel. She will read and read and write and write and so travel many writerly miles. It is a new form of writing, practical, pragmatic and away from home.

Her journals from this period of her life are full of records of places and the movement between them. Places visited, extended sojourns, the seven weeks of the summer holiday: these are the capsules of time and place Virginia stores away in her diary now-turned-journal. 'We settle into a very free out of door life,' she declares.[52] This is what it means to go on holiday.

*

If we think of a journal as a record of an extended period of time in a particular place, then Woolf's writings from the early 1900s are journals rather than diaries. In her journals, the diary's everydayness becomes more elastic: places, rather than dates, set experience. There are other benefits: place brings more furniture, physical mementoes, the opportunity for souvenirs. By the end of her adolescence, by the time she is twenty-one, Woolf's journals have become miniature museums of experience. The question now is where to store them. She turns to books as the most reliable storage space. Books are more reliable than people, for books are more likely to endure.

Holidays require more pragmatic methods of journaling. But this is not a new method; she has been practising this for some time. Four years before, during the annual family holiday in St Ives, Cornwall, seventeen-year-old Virginia began this, her scrapbook method of journaling. She reports this 'sudden idea' to her journal: she will bury the pages of her journal inside 'the leaves of some worthy & ancient work' and so embed the life of her writing within the life of something ancient. Thus her journal pages will fossilise, gather age and strength. They will mature.

On a visit to 'the old curiosity shop' in St Ives, an old antique shop, she alights upon a copy of Isaac Watts's *LOGICK: OR THE Right Use of REASON*, etc, bound in leather. This old book will be her storage chest, her book-chest, her paper-closet. Her new method will be one of 'desecration' of the old: she will rip out the pages of Sir Isaac Watt's *LOGICK* and furnish it with her own handwritten pages of notes on places, people and things.[53] She will build her own memory book from the shell of some old form of knowledge. Woolf will desecrate the work of 'logick' and rebuild it from the illogical jumble of her own memories and experiences.

Well-weathered Places

Diaries can cultivate intense memories of places and time beyond the everyday world. Like many writers, Woolf is a fan of the sojourn or visit. But not all sojourns are carefree or chosen; some are recuperative. Woolf's 1917 diary, for example, is distinctly restorative, as empty of people as it is slight of build: a small notebook of 65 pages, 15½ centimetres by 10. Her 'Asheham diary', named after her first Sussex house, was to remain in situ, a small notebook she returned and added to on later visits.[54] Asheham, then, enjoys a distinct pre-eminence in the diarist's imagination. It is of a regular and fixed abode. Asheham is her first home away from London, which she shared with her new husband, Leonard Woolf.

Sojourning in Sussex in the late summer of that year, Woolf records the condition of the sky as a means of getting her day started. Inclement weather is often code for a faltering start, and in this, her Asheham diary, begun two years after an extended breakdown and during a summer of fragile mental health, the often trepidations beginnings of her entries indicate someone who has forgotten her place in life; how exactly to start her day. In the late summer of 1917, Virginia Stephen, now Woolf, is finding it hard to speak even to her diary.

Talk of the weather breaks the ice. Clouds seem to prompt thinking, and from here, Woolf turns back to the events of the day:

> *Monday 3 September*
> Perfect day; completely blue without cloud or wind, as if settled for ever. Watched dog herding sheep. Rooks beginning to fly over the trees … sometimes with starlings … Evening fine so we went out again into the hollow. Saw a shining spot, which we could not find when we came up it. Painted Lady [*Vanessa cardui*] seen near Glynde.[55]

As a diarist, this is not her finest moment, and indeed the entries surrounding this one are rather sparse, more a series of jottings than complete thoughts. Consisting mainly of glimpses, rather than steady observations, the Asheham diary suggests a scattered and depleted mind. Woolf can look up at the sky and down at the ground, but she cannot record anything in between. These are landscape sketches with missing middle spaces; there is nothing on the horizon because Woolf does not know what will come next. Time and space and their potential subjects are all missing from her canvas. There is no narrative. Woolf can manage nature's details but not the human plot. People and parties are forgotten. Dinner is an afterthought.

Woolf's Asheham diary begins in early August 1917 and ends in early October the same year, and while the events seem faint and rather wispy – threadbare happenings, rather than solid events – clouds dominate.

But why pay such attention to the sky? Perhaps because clouds connote atmosphere and lend shape and tone to the sky, elements often missing from the days described. Indeed, many of these entries hang purely upon clouds: 'We went to get blackberries on top ... A cloud over the land all day, except late in the evening, when the sun came out beneath it in an odd way.'[56] The cloud 'over the land all day' reads as a kind of celestial prophecy. A few days later, Woolf paints a small land-scape framed by clouds:

> An almost motionless day; no blue sky; almost like a win-ter day, save for the heat. Very quiet. Over to picnic at Firle in the afternoon. Nessa & 5 children came after we had done; sat outside the trees. Walked home over the downs. Red sky over the sea. Woods almost as thin as winter, but very little colour in them.[57]

The entry reads as a miniature postcard, an aerial view of the Downs around Lewes and Glynde, between the Woolfs' house and her sister's across the Down. There is a kind of symmetry to the above and below life of these Downland passages, each part – sky and land – drifting loosely along.

The plot is loose and impressionstic, drifting. A picnic at Firle takes place among trees. Vanessa, Woolf's sister, and her children join the arrangement of people, trees and sky. But no one really seems to be in charge. The voice of the writing has disappeared. Woolf's subjectless sentences suggest absent-mindedness. With no 'I' to put things in order, the passages read more like a series of doodles. These are loose sketches rather than gathered thoughts, a scrubland of sentences bare of subjects and syntax. We experience snatches of place, impressions of moments. Figures and forms are few. We amble through atmospheric effects of colour, light and tone.

*

Diary writing requires 'a little jagged piece of time', away from the crowds, Woolf notes.[58] For most of her adult writing life, Virginia Woolf was moving back and forth between Sussex and London. In 1919 Asheham House in Sussex was replaced by her second Sussex house: Monk's House at Rodmell, near Lewes. Sussex seems to produce more writing, London more reading and, naturally, more parties and talk.

It is fair to say that the diaries Woolf wrote in London have a distinctly different tone from the entries she makes in Sussex. In Sussex, her mind drifts along at a different pace, moving through 'spaces of leisure'; here she stops snatching, grabbing and consuming experience the way she does in London.[59] Sussex drifts along through clouds and rain; it offers a differ-ent writing environment, another climate of thought. Woolf's diary mentality shifts and alters accordingly.

A London entry quite often begins with the appraisal of a party, a piece adorned with snippets of conversation: 'Back again in London. A party last night: Mary Fisher, Eddie Playfair, Rose Macaulay & Saxon. An odd mixture; but successful. We cried with laughter.' Woolf continues to cut and paste scraps of conversation, creating a version of a parlour game.[60] She is amusing herself while remembering her friends fondly. Here is intimacy without privacy, a kind of coterie consciousness.

City Sojourns

In November 1762, Woolf's diary-ancestor, twenty-two-year-old James Boswell, future author of the first great biography in English, *The Life of Samuel Johnson*, was setting forth on a trip to London. On the eve of his departure he begins a journal. He sets out his intentions:

> I have therefore determined to keep a daily journal in which I set down my various sentiments and my various conduct, which will be not only very useful, but very agreeable. It will give me a habit of application and improve me in expression; and knowing that I am to record my transactions will make me more careful to do well.[61]

Boswell's statement of purpose reads more like a job description or an apprenticeship: his journal will lend a form of discipline for a young man 'about town'. It will provide him with a means of improving his self-expression and enable him to consider his conduct and 'transactions' with the world. It will be a place for gathering thoughts and opinions on people and places. Finally, it is somewhere he can set down the anecdotes, stories and conversation he is 'present at'. His journal will provide the young man with a mode of assessing himself and the world around him.[62] It will turn him into a social anthropologist.

Boswell's journal has a lot to live up to. As son of stern Scottish judge, Lord Auchinleck, patriarch of the ancient Auchinleck estate in Ayrshire, he will need his journal to help him fend off accusations from his father of dissipation and idleness, profligacy and drunkenness.[63] His journal will act as a safeguard to his filial reputation. It will help him manage his fraught relationship with his father.

Boswell also writes, as he tells us, for the sake of his dear friend John Johnston of Grange to whom he sends the entire journal in weekly parcels.[64] Johnston, then, vicariously benefits from Boswell's encounter with character and conversation; and it is Johnston's blessing and best wishes Boswell looks for before he departs. But Johnston is not at home and Boswell commences his journey to London without bidding farewell to his friend to whom he will serve, from a distance, as journalistic alter ego.[65] His journal is left to bridge the distance between himself and his friend, to generate conversation across time and space.[66]

Live and organic, conversation is an ephemeral form of life, and the best conversation often proves too rich and heady in the moment to be easily remembered. Conversation itself creates a kind of locality; it marks a place between two or more people, a beginning and an ending. It is a kind of journey into new forms of knowledge and experience. Good conversation carries us forward. On arriving in London, and at the recommendation of his father, he seeks out the company of Lord Eglinton, who is expecting him and greets him generously. And so Boswell finds himself ushered into the company of members of the peerage, men of 'great genius, great knowledge, and much whim'.[67] These are men who can teach him about the world.

Shared interests spark good dialogue, and it is good dialogue that lies at the heart of Boswell's journal. Just as he prides himself on being good company, so Boswell is concerned not to bore his journal with too much formality. That is no way to entertain a friend. 'To go regularly through the day would be too formal for my journal. Besides, every day cannot be passed exactly the same way in every particular.'[68] His journal watches Boswell as Boswell passes his days. Certainly, there is a sense of accountability. But this is not the parental censure of Lord Auchinleck, but something more companionable.

*

His meeting with Dr Johnson on May 16th 1763, in the back parlour of his friend Thomas Davis, was to bring him the big event he needed. All at once, his journal had access to the best material on offer: the witty repartee of the legendary doctor, compiler of *The Dictionary of the English Language*, and the best conversationalist in town. The effect on Boswell of this first meeting was enormous. His journal suddenly had a purpose and a patron. Johnson had blessed the project; what better purpose could there be than to fill his journal with all the 'strength of sentiment and perspicuity of expression' that characterised the doctor's conversation?[69] What is more, Johnson's conversation is a direct line to the public world and public discourse. It marks the beginning of Boswell's future project, his great biography of the doctor. Following that first meeting, he makes a promise to himself. From now on, he shall 'just mark Mr. Johnson's memorabilia as they rise up in my memory, observing however, as much as convenient the times at which they were observed'.[70]

Johnson has given the younger man a method for evaluating life. He has endorsed his journal:

He advised me to keep a journal of my life, fair and un-
disguised. He said it would be a very good exercise, and
would yield me infinite satisfaction when the ideas were
faded from my remembrance. I told him that I had done
so ever since I left Scotland. He said he was very happy
that I pursued so good a plan. And now, O my journal!
Art thou not dignified? Shalt thou not flourish tenfold?
No former solicitations or censures could tempt me to lay
thee aside; and now is there any argument which can out-
weigh the sanction of Mr. Samuel Johnson?[71]

Johnson sanctions the journal idea as a concerned father might
support a nurturing friendship. It is to be Boswell's better and
more reliable self, an aide-mémoire that will fill the gaps in his
life story he might otherwise forget. Boswell's journal will
provide him both with an itinerary, a 'good plan', and a travelling companion. He will bear witness to all his achievements.

*

By August 1763, Boswell has found his purpose and he is
ready to leave. His London sojourn has greatly improved his
prospects. Writing on his last London day he reflects upon
his enhanced state:

4 August 1763
This is now my last day in London before I set out upon
my travels, and makes a very important period in my
journal. Let me recollect my life since this journal began.
Has it not passed like a dream? Yes, but I have been
attaining a knowledge of the world. I came to town to go
into the Guards. How different is my scheme now! I am

upon a less pleasurable but a more rational and lasting plan. Let me pursue it with steadiness and I may be a man of dignity. My mind is strangely agitated. I am happy to think of going upon my travels and seeing the diversity of foreign parts; and yet my feeble mind shrinks somewhat at the idea of leaving Britain in so very short a time from the moment in which I now make this remark. How strange must I feel myself in foreign parts. My mind too is gloomy and dejected at the thoughts of leaving London, where I am so comfortably situated and where I have enjoyed most happiness. However, I shall be the happier for being abroad, as long as I live. Let me be manly. Let me commit myself to the care of my merciful creator. [72]

Boswell now has a 'new scheme', an adjusted character and a more distinct view of the world. His London days have settled him down; he no longer 'rattles' like an old carriage but has acquired something more 'composed' and 'genteel'. [73] He is leaving with a character better formed and more informed. He is ready to give up the extraordinary moment that has been London and Johnson, until the next time.

Boswell leaves London but not his journal. After nearly nine months, the city has yielded enough life, and by the beginning of August 1763 it is time to move on. [74] In Johnson he has acquired a mentor and guide, friend, companion and teacher. He will take himself to 'foreign parts' to test his new 'scheme'. His journal will go with him and spur him on to an identity beyond the doctor, beyond his familiar friends and his ruinous habits. [75]

Foreign Places

Historically speaking, diaries have played the role of reliable witness to foreign places. The Renaissance philosopher Francis Bacon urged all travellers to 'make diaries' in order to secure details of their experience for posterity.[76] Human memory is a precarious thing, subject to all sorts of distortions and forms of corruption. We remember what we want to remember; we edit and we alter.

Philosopher John Locke, the inheritor of Bacon's empirical pedagogy, argued that knowledge is determined by experience.[77] But experience must be recorded in order to have any lasting effect. Locke was himself a disciplined keeper of a commonplace book, a version of the journal that functioned more as a notebook for storing edifying thoughts and phrases. Here was a way of creating a network of knowledge in which curation was everything. Carefully selected words arranged serendipitously on the page could lead to surprising associations.[78] Locke's commonplace book generated a new method of indexing experience by listing categories of similar-sounding words: 'Beauty, Beneficence, Bread'.[79] Such phonetic lists might prompt a frail memory and resuscitate valued experience: observations, conversation and quotations worth remembering. Locke, as Emerson was later to agree, believed that 'sensation' was the key to felt experience.[80] You feel and so you know, but what you know lies partly beyond or around you.

The commonplace book, like the journal and the Grand Tour, forms part of an eighteenth-century culture of male self-improvement. It is another early ancestor of the self-help book. Students of the commonplace book and journal were

34

loosely following the methods prescribed by Samuel Johnson: go somewhere worth seeing and keep a journal account of the best parts. Create the best record of yourself in the world as you can. Boswell does precisely this.

*

Ten years on from leaving London, Boswell finally agrees to a tour of Scotland with his old friend. Boswell's *Journal of a Tour to the Hebrides* (August to November 1773) begins as a deliberate search for the unfamiliar. Advised that travel will develop the 'dignity' of his character, he convinces himself of the need to sally forth into the unknown. But Boswell is not really travelling into the unknown; he goes to the Hebrides with Johnson and their familiar habits of conversation. Boswell takes both Johnson and his journal. The two seem inseparable, as indeed they will eventually become, wed to posterity in Boswell's *The Life of Samuel Johnson*, begun shortly after Johnson's death in 1794.

Journal of a Tour (published 1785) is the beginning of that biography, built upon 'prized specimens' of conversation, and for the reader it seems close to a naturalist's notebook or an entomologist's net: it works hard to capture a living creature. The dramatic landscapes of the Hebrides are often subordinate to the great doctor, 'subordination' being Johnson's favourite topic.[81] Indeed, the entire journal is led by the sound of Johnson's voice, directing the journey as he ushers his student into documentary exercises. Johnson is guide and mentor, captain and teacher.

Landing upon the island of Inchkeith in the Firth of Forth, Johnson asks Boswell to write a full account of the place in the style of a travelogue or anthropologist's notebook: he should catalogue the particular features of the island and so excite the curiosity of future travellers. Boswell is given homework; he must make 'sage reflections' and draw conclusions, based on local observation and research. His journal will do the work of natural history.

Around all this careful reportage lurks the character and personality of Johnson himself, stalking the place like a rare species: difficult to pin down but perpetually fascinating. Here is the real history. Johnson's gestures and phrases circulate like the local customs, and as the pair leave Inchkeith he calls out to Boswell to pay the island a 'classical compliment'.[82] Small rituals and gestures mark out one place from another, creating a sequence of symbolic arrivals and departures equivalent to the date and place of Boswell's journal entries. Boswell writes, and Johnson expounds. Boswell notes and records, and Johnson delivers an epithet or witty summary. Johnson knows everything already; he is pure tradition and pure custom, a body of experience that has stood the test of time: part fossil, part living.

Reading the *Journal of a Tour* we are struck by how much Johnson becomes Scotland, its flora and fauna, its geology and geography; just how much Boswell defers to the doctor for seeing and knowing the country. Like Robinson Crusoe's Man Friday, Johnson is an incarnate version of Boswell's journal; he is experience heavily mediated by the personal, place wrapped around the anecdote. Of course the journal is far more a journey into biography than it is into Scotland itself, a reminder of the close borders between journals and life-writing.

Knowledge consistently takes the form of anecdotes; and so crossing from the port of Leith, Edinburgh to Inchkeith, Johnson regales Boswell and his servant with tales of Boswell's ancestors, the Lairds of Auchinleck, who, he tells us, fought in the Civil War barefooted. Both men begin to wax lyrical on ancestral history. Boswell is ecstatic about the view across the Firth, comparing it to the view over Constantinople – which he has never seen – and then about Naples, which he has. In the middle of all this tall talk and myth-making, Boswell presses for a glorified appraisal of his home town. Edinburgh must have a place in these myths too. The view of Edinburgh is also impressive, he reminds his companion. Johnson corrects this view with a witty epigram: 'Ay... that is the state of the world. Water is the same everywhere.' The younger man is sufficiently chastened. Johnson's advice is that he should forget home, forget the Scotland that he knows.[83] He must bury himself in new forms of enchantment and above all he must remember that the doctor has the last word.

Travel encourages fickleness. En route we forget our past commitments and conventions, our old loyalties. As we embrace new terrain, we adopt new attitudes and leave the old ones behind. We fall in love with where we are. Our view of things may not be reliable. Travellers are natural romantics as they are often uncommitted lovers. By extension, travel journals encourage the fickle and the fey, fleeting forms of self.

Reviewing and Renewing

But we also go abroad to review what we have left at home. On New Year's Eve 1955, twenty-three-year-old Sylvia Plath travelled to the Mediterranean to settle her history with her former lover Richard Sassoon. She leaves behind 'gray Cambridge' and 'gray London' and goes in search of sunshine, colour and sensuality. Her journal fragment from this brief period is a study of colour, form and light. Everything she sees becomes a painting. Plath is a travelling empiricist and, in the tradition of empirical observation, her journal converts what she sees into a sequence of sensory compositions built around light, shape and sound. Travel is a painterly exercise that leads her away from the pall of England.

Travel brings rhythms: the movement of the train pulling out of the Gare de Lyon, Paris; breathless figures rushing down the platform; Christmas tree lights blinking out a Morse code through the window – a rhythm waiting for those who wait and watch. Plath's journal is a holdall of visual prompts and props; between herself and Cambridge, she stacks up a large amount of visual luggage – suitcase after suitcase – until the grey memories of that town are obliterated. Cambridge and England are folded away inside a mental map of France she conjures up as she moves. Movement develops imagery better than anything, and Plath knows this. Her train journey is preparation for seeing things more intensely – in passing, flushed by the adrenalin of high speed:

At last, the shriek of whistles, the yell of porters and the moment of intuitive silence. The train began to move. Off into the night, with the blackness of a strange land knifing past. In my mind, a map of France, irregularly squarish, with a minute Eiffel Tower marking Paris towards the north, and a line of railway tracks, like a zipper, speeding open to the south, to Marseille, to Nice and the Cote d'Azur where perhaps in the realm of absolute fact the sun is shining and the sky is turquoise. Away from the sodden mud and cutting winds of gray Cambridge, away from the freezing white frosts of cold gray London where the sun hung in the white mists like a bloody egg yolk. Away from the rain and wet feet of Paris, with colored lights wavering in the gutters running with water and the Seine flowed gray and sluggish by the quais and Notre Dame lifted two towers to a lowering, thick, curded gray sky.[84]

Plath is mixing a new palette and building a new composition for herself. The train journey prompts mental travel, but more than this, the opportunity to refurbish imagery of mind and place. Her journey is an internal overhauling of her mind, the replacing of the map of England with that of France, and replacing Hughes, her husband-to-be, with Sassoon.

In some sense, Sassoon is the journey. Plath's journey into France is meditative, hypnotic almost: an obliteration of the near present. She reaches for the powerful present, as Boswell reaches for the present tense, in the hope that he will be more faithful to the dramatic moment.[85] Plath moves rapidly south, unpeeling aspects of herself and her culture that no longer suit her.

*

Four months later she visits Paris again, this time in flight from a terrible row with her husband-to-be, Ted Hughes. Once again, Plath goes to France to paint words: layer upon layer of thick word-tempera. Words obliterate the memory of Hughes, the artist she leaves behind. Travel is now a remedy for loss, and her journal a log of loss. What has been lost is the first flush of love. Plath is confused, emotionally in limbo. She and Hughes now have history between them; and history is not always comfortable. Paris is Sassoon, but as Sassoon is nowhere to be found, Plath has to make do with another flame, Gordon Lameyer, who suggests they visit Rome.

Her trip becomes a 'smorgasbord' of men in different European capitals: Sassoon in Paris, or not in Paris; Gordon in Rome, or not in Rome; Ted in London, and in between men called Gary, Tony and Giovanni who fill her journal like a catalogue of well-spent days.[86] It is 'Ted' who dominates these journal entries, late March 1956; and it is Ted she is to marry in June 1956 – three and a half months later. In reality, Plath has only spent a few days with Ted, but at this point in her young life she is still measuring life in days, not months or even years. Her holocaust row with Ted is a single night. The history between them is very slight. She still doesn't know quite how Ted 'talks' but she would like to know.[87]

In the end, this part of Plath's European journal is far more committed to return than it is to being away. It is the sound of Ted she hankers after: it is Ted she wants to know, not Paris, Rome or Munich. Her journey away from London is more to do with emotional resettlement than a desire to see foreign places. Paris, Nice, Rome, Munich: this is all time out. Ted is the real foreign experience she craves. Meanwhile, her journal allows her to circle and calculate the equations of her particular choices. Everything is considered but contingent: a maybe, a could, a what if. She hesitates over her future like a novice prophet.

Her final April 1956 entry from Paris is surrounded with 'auguries' of 'departure', a fateful language. Her Paris bathroom is turning grey around the edges. This space, this interval of time is closing down to her, that is to say her most recent alternative, Gordon Lameyer. Her journal becomes a 'fatal dance' through which she weaves and revolves the choices of her thinking, calculating self:

Ted can break walls; I could telegraph him tonight if I could come home to London and live there till Whitstead ... there is so little time; tonight all must happen; before 7 when I meet Gordon: he just now is the safest way: I would conquer two countries (and however much I want to linger in Italy; is it not better to see five days and come back hungry to stay longer, having foraged first under a man's protection, still off season, able to explore without pickups?). ah yes. If Richard would come back now... [88]

Plath writes compelling melodrama. Emotional forms are absurdly large and loud and, potentially, everything 'could' or 'would' mean something if only Plath dared it to. Action hangs in suspense, in what Plath grandly calls 'the historic moment', the moment of 'her', whoever or whatever that will be.

Plath travels in order to settle upon a role and a context for what she visualises as the rest of her life. Her journal travels with her as an unofficial witness of an unofficial contract: a document commissioned to produce the workings of her future self. As Dr Johnson eloquently put it, the use of travel is to 'regulate imagination by reality, and instead of thinking how things may be, to see them as they are'. [89] Contemporary travellers may still be looking for a way to reassess themselves, as twenty-four-year-old Plath did on her way to Paris. But the modern world, as travel blogger Ari N. Schulman reminds us, offers so many opportunities for us to remain the same. We may be in the Australian outback, but, imaginatively, we have travelled nowhere. We get online and we email our friends back home. We check up on the state of play between this relationship and that. We ask, How is the cat? Did you remember to lock the back door at night? Is there any food left in the freezer? We have not, as novelist Walker Percy writes, met with the 'genie-soul' of the place.[90]

My Travel Journal

The second time I was sent abroad I knew how to use a camera, or very nearly. I packed a camera, a notebook and three rolls of film. My notebook, or journal as I preferred to call it – this time a soft, grey, furry thing – was filled with French vocabulary: 'Où se trouve la gare?' 'Où se trouve la toilette?' 'Où se trouve la maison?' 'Où se trouve la boulangerie?' 'Où se trouve la fromagerie?' 'Où se trouve l'école?' French, I decided, was only for people who were lost. But I'd been told never to get lost. So when was I ever going to use it? 'Stick with an adult,' my mother said; 'stick with an adult if you're not sure about anything. And for goodness' sake listen. Then you won't get lost.' French was also for people who didn't listen.

I went back to Switzerland to stay with relatives of the first family, the Grosjean family, which in French means Large John. Large John, I thought, must be a relative of Little John. It was a funny name to call an entire family.

But everyone in Switzerland was related to someone else and they all spoke French, Italian or German, a funny sort of German. Languages passed to and fro like the big bowl of pasta that Madame Grosjean served every lunchtime (who was Italian even though she had a French name). Every morning, after choc-au-lait, in the kitchen with the high windows and long wooden table, I pulled out my notebook and added more names to the list of pastas Madame Grosjean had taught me: 'spaghetti', 'cannelloni', 'conchiglioni', 'conchigliette' (which was a smaller sort of 'conchiglioni'), 'fusilli', 'fettucine', 'gemelli'.

My eyes bulged at the words, strange insects, those slugs or snails, crossing the page. How could anyone possibly eat anything called 'conchiglioni'? But I wanted to remember the size and shape of those foreign curls that sat squirming on my plate, those little soft things covered in butter or cheese. I wouldn't be able to remember them as they were; to remember the shiny pink mouths of Monsieur and Madame Grosjean as they pushed silver forkfuls inside them, while 'jabbering away nineteen to the dozen' as my grandmother would say, in a language that sounded like French wrapped around Italian, sliced through with German (German only when they were swallowing). It would have been rude to take photographs then as they spoke about 'la famille' and 'mariage' and 'le méchant garçon' and 'la petite', who I think was me.

I wanted to remember what the pasta looked like when people weren't eating it. 'Cannelloni', 'conchiglioni', 'gemelli': a different pasta for every day. Where could I use these words? I would never be able to say them properly. Monday was a 'fusilli' day, Tuesday a 'fettucine', Wednesday a 'gemelli'; lundi – fusilli, mardi – fettucine, mercredi – gemelli. I could learn the days of the weeks by pasta. Every pasta would have a different colour, a different Caran-d'Ache pencil colour: sky blue, lavender-purple, moss green. But I ran out of colours and got confused when I tried to label them in my journal. So I decided to take photos instead. I took out one piece from each of the glass bottles Madame Grosjean kept in the kitchen and laid them out on a large plate with plenty of white space in between. Then I sat at the end of the long table and leaned towards them with my elbows on the table top, balancing my camera, trying to hold it perfectly still. But it kept moving. 'Click, click, click.' The table wobbled on top of the slippery flagged floors; the pasta slid forward, rolling away from me. I tipped further over the table, lifting up my leg, then my skirt, wrapping my foot around the twisty table leg.

Madame Grosjean found me when she came in to do the ironing and laughed. She laughed so loud I thought she was going to explode. Her body tipped over in half, folded down the middle. She looked like a paper cut-out doll. 'Qu'est-ce que tu fais, ma petite?' Another question. But I wasn't lost. I was doing something important: I was recording things for my journal so I could remember exactly what had happened. Eating pasta, after all, was the main thing. That was what I'd done every day since I arrived. That was what you did if you lived in Switzerland with an Italian mother who made fresh pasta from a machine with a silver handle she turned and turned as though she were pumping water from a well. But instead of water, long flat strips of pale dough came out; it never stopped. It just kept coming and coming as Madame Grosjean's arms rose up and down. I could see the muscles in her upper arms poking through like Popeye with his shirt open and his sleeves rolled up to impress Olive Oyl.

I wanted to take a photo of Madame Grosjean, so I sidled off to my bedroom and found my camera and stood behind her and clicked. 'La petite! Qu'est-ce que tu fais?' Madame Grosjean didn't like her photo being taken. Neither did I. But I had to have something to put in my journal and I didn't know how to translate what I saw from the sound of French and Italian buzzing in my ears all day long. If I had some pictures I could remember things more clearly.

But photographs were unreliable and there was always a

delay. You couldn't see what you'd taken, so you had no idea whether the pictures were any good or not – until it was too late. You had to wait until you got back home and Mum took them to Boots to be developed, which meant handing them over to the man with the white coat who grinned at you as though he knew that your snaps wouldn't be very good. He'd take my photos home and laugh and smirk at my botched efforts to reproduce what I saw on my plate. 'Why would anyone take photos of pasta on holiday?' he would say to his wife in bed that night. 'Why would you go all the way to France, or Italy, or Switzerland just to take photographs of bits of pasta on a plate?'

'It's probably a school project, dear. You know how it is these days ... they have to write everything down ... turn it into a real experience ... write up what they see ... pretend they're journalists ... pretend they're real people with something to say. I think it's quite good really ... more useful than writing out lines from Shakespeare none of us understood. Of course they don't have much to say at their age, bless them. But I think it's better than that old-fashioned rubbish.'

'Well, I don't know what on earth you'd say about a few bits of pasta.'

And by the time I got back home, neither did I.

*

Pepys, though he does leave London, never really meets with any other place. When we read Pepys's diary we are aware that although he sails across the Channel to Holland, as a crucial part of Charles II's water taxi, mentally he remains at home.

London is Pepys and Pepys is London. He rarely leaves the

place. Virginia Woolf rarely leaves England, and when she does, it comes as a response to a terrible loss.

But losses and gains are the operative forces of travel. When Woolf leaves England, she does so as a means of recalibrating her life in the aftermath of a terrible loss. In April 1932, the year Sylvia Plath was born, Plath's self-acknowledged literary foremother, Virginia Woolf, prepares to leave London for Greece following the death of her close friend and fellow critic and aesthete, Lytton Strachey.[91]

You might say that Woolf travels, as Plath is also to do, in order to decide which people or persons remaining matter most to her. In Paris, Plath says goodbye to old flames; she closes a significant chapter of her young history. In 1932 and as a woman twice Plath's age, Woolf is undertaking a similar emotional journey. She travels to Athens to re-establish intimacy among her remaining friends. Travel offers relief from the climate of grief that has settled upon her like a thick fog. She can no longer think, and her diary entries leading up to her departure marry the weather with what she calls her 'muddle headed[ness]'.[92]

But Greece is not just a getaway; it is also a review of her youth – Athens being the place she had visited as a young woman of twenty-three. Athens is also surrounded by memories of death: of her brother, Thoby, who died shortly after the first Greek trip, in 1906. Greece, then, is tragedy and loss, and in Athens she reviews aspects of her former self, painting over as she revises the original canvas hanging in her memory. Her painter's wash is distinctly elegiac. In the ancient ruins, she meets with her 'own ghost', 'the girl of 23, with all her life to come'. She remembers things differently. The photographic wash that coloured those earlier days has a different tint. Things are 'more splendid & robust' than she remembered.

She hesitates to find the right words, the correct image to describe the Parthenon the second time round. It is larger than Woolf remembered and in better shape; it is more yellow.

Woolf washes down the old canvas and begins to recompose what she sees now rather than what she remembers. Her diary shuttles between stored views of the past and the present, performing the sort of memory work that allows ghosts of her former self to settle and breathe – then move on. 'How shall I say', asks Woolf, as she tries to describe the Parthenon to her diary; how shall she say now, rather than then? 'Gathered and grouped', her memories 'radiate' from the yellow surface of the temple. Like any good tourist, her diary takes snapshots, for what else is there to remember a trip by? She is obliged to recall what is 'still' there, after years have passed, and what was only imagined.[93] And so the camera's eye of her diary, fearing that the moment may pass, keeps on clicking.

Orcadia, August 1985

My family was too large to go on holiday together. Family holidays are for a mum, a dad, two children and perhaps a dog. Babies can go on holiday if they sleep a lot. I can't remember exactly how many babies there were in my family by the summer of 1985. Babies were being born all the time.

In August 1985 (my birthday month) my family took a trip to the Orkney Islands. Orkney, if you don't know, is at the furthest tip of Scotland, facing north. And you don't have to call it 'the Orkney Islands' or 'the Orkneys' as my aunt did. People who come from Orkney are called Orcadians, and so I thought that logically 'Orkney' should be called 'Orcadia'. 'Orcadia' was the word I wrote in my diary from that holiday. 'Orcadia' was the title I wrote at the top of the first page. 'Orcadia' was the name of the small marine-blue book I stowed away inside my clothes. 'Orcadia' was where I was going.

Orcadia looks over towards Scandinavia, which means Norway and Sweden and then maybe Iceland. By the time you got to Orcadia you are only 575 miles away from Norway, going north. To me, Orcadia was the end of the world. The sky and the sea of Orcadia are the same steely grey; the sea and the sky are the same thing: the sea is the sky and the sky is the sea.

I wrote that in my diary because it frightened me. I was used to the sea being blue-green and the sky being mostly white. At home there was the pale yellow sand, the blue-green sea, the white sky with grey tufts and some flecks of blue. Everything was clear and distinct. Here, in Orcadia, although there was wind blowing all the time, it was hard to breathe because the wind was so fierce and hard. It punched you in the stomach and sent you towards the sea.

There was no way out between the end of the sea and the start of the sky. I kept looking for the end of the sea but I couldn't see it. I wanted to see a seam, an edge, a ridge. 'Where is the end of the sea?' I asked my diary. 'How can you tell where you're going here? How do the Orcadian children live without sun? It is always grey. How do they go swimming in the sea?'

*

Going to the Orkneys meant a big hullabaloo. This is what my grandmother said. It meant 16 people on a train and then a plane, a tiny little plane that took us from mainland Scotland over the grey sea. My aunt wouldn't take the boat, and in any case we would have sunk it, all those people with all their stuff, the hull bumping and scraping along the sea floor.

We took a lot to Orcadia: our cat and rabbit, my grandmother, my three brothers, my seven cousins and one baby. Then my mum and aunt and their friend Angie. Angie was there to help carry all the stuff. I carried a small suitcase for my brother Daniel and me and I stuffed it with treasures. I hid things on the bottom of my suitcase in case it fell into the sea. I thought that if I put things on the very bottom then no one would see them even if they drowned. So I wrapped my diary inside the pocket of my blue jumpsuit, my electric-blue jumpsuit that turned me into a blue spark in all the videos my aunt took of us. I put my blue jumpsuit at the bottom of my suitcase and it looked like the sea floor.

*

When I think of our holiday in Orcadia I always see the dark shadow of a video camera; the endless filming of us blowing about near low sea-walls; gaggles of small children being silly in front of the camera; my brothers and cousins saying as many rude things as possible without my aunt hearing; small boys burping and armpit-farting and sticking their fingers in their mouths like lollipops and giggling. They got away with it because the wind was on their side, because the wind was blowing their words away into the sea.

That holiday was when I began to disappear. I'm in almost none of the footage my aunt brought back: the hours and hours of wind and sky and stone walls; my mother walking around the edge of low fields outside our motel with Washington the cat on a lead; my mother with her hair nudged

49

to one side; and my aunt patrolling the edges of the frame in a mottled purple dress. 'Off-lavender', she called it; the colour of grey meeting purple after the purple has almost all run out; the colour of sagging eyelids on dead people.

Years later when I play a snatch of those films to my brother Daniel, I see myself flicker on and off the screen like a blue ghost. I don't look at the camera. I don't turn my head the way they want me. I won't look their way. It is August 1985 and I'm a twelve-year-old girl desperately looking for solitude, looking for somewhere to hide from the sea and sky, the heavy grey clouds, the low-lying atmosphere, the relentless gaze of the camera eye.

CHAPTER THREE

BACK TO NATURE

Woolf returns from Greece to Monk's House, Sussex, where she rehabilitates herself in the English countryside. For a moment, the landscapes of Greece and England stand side by side, before Greece disappears into the Sussex Downs. She starts to see England again. But before her Greek eyes disappear, Woolf arranges and edits the photographic 'visions' she has gathered. She revisits the Parthenon temple, rehearses the routes she took in Aegina and Athens, crystallises the views she took in. She 'brings forward' the images of Greece like a moving slide show, a turning carousel she hopes will eventually produce 'detached pictures that will stand alone in her mind'.[94] Greece must stand apart from England.

Woolf's diary treats views – or in her more ecstatic language 'visions' – as specimens. The Greek landscape is something to be caught and captured, pursued even, to use the language of the naturalist Woolf often applied to her daily sightings. Writing her biography of her beloved friend Roger Fry, Woolf casts herself in the role of naturalist chasing down her fluttering specimen: 'I can't help thinking I've caught a great deal of that iridescent man in my oh so laborious butterfly net,'[95] she smugly declares. Woolf was adamant that she must pin him down only to truthful representations. Her diary was a container for the 'iridescent' flare of close observation – the peer of the naturalist – that her novels, essays and reviews could not reach. At its most august, it is an anthropological museum of people and places, types of experience, a more accurate lens by which to view 'life itself', that is to say the living specimen, 'going on'.[96]

*

Thrown back into London life, Woolf treasures her weekends in Rodmell, her 'fortnightly dip' into the colours and contours of Sussex.[97] English gardens revive her. She begins to look again with English eyes. Rodmell is 'deep safe book reading' and sleep; it is also the garden with its 'mounds of green' and the may tree outside her bedroom window 'like a breaking wave'. In Rodmell, Woolf climbs into 'green tunnels': nature surrounds and encloses her and the Rodmell diary is filled with references to her sensory tunnelling into the 'vapours' and 'green caverns' of her garden.[98]

Clouds, rain, sunshine, trees, fields, flowers: this is as much the stuff of Woolf's journals as it is people and parties, reviews and proofs, ideas for novels and the goings-on among her servants. Nature is space for thinking; it nurtures open-mindedness, a more elastic view of experience. As we have already seen, cloudy skies are recuperative sights. They encourage imaginative suggestions. Beyond the hurried and harried world of domestic chores and cramped timing, nature lends its own order. Woolf sits in Kew Gardens with Leonard and finds a composition waiting for her: life going on unarranged and undetermined. The natural spectacle, the robins and the squirrels beneath the tree, simply give her something else to think about.[99] Her mind can wander and stretch out, make new associations. Nature, along with her diary, offers a blank canvas for free thinking, for rambling and roaming. The nature diarist is a free thinker.

*

Nature is 'ample and roomy', declared American naturalist philosopher Henry David Thoreau. 'She has left us plenty of space to move in.' Thoreau, who began his journal in 1837, aged twenty, spends much of his life as a philosopher and writer considering the benefits of nature to human life. What good, he wonders, does it do to spend so much time in the company of flowers and trees?

One answer is that nature makes us larger than ourselves; she draws us out and away from our diminishing habits. As a committed introvert, Thoreau understood this. His chief companion was nature, and his journal is a report on how he and nature spend time together on particular days.

If we read Thoreau's journal 'roomy', we note, means the sound of bees, a live soundscape of humming that opens up the airwaves; a gladed wood is also 'roomy', but the ultimate experience of roominess is the sight of the horizon.[100] Where earth and sky meet, there is the contact point between the imaginative and the actual.[101] In some way, this is a metaphor for what the journal performs.

At the end of the day the horizon, like Thoreau's journal, firmly underscores the end of the daily cycle but with the knowledge that more will come tomorrow. Gazing out from the window of his home, Thoreau is glad to see emptiness. Unpeopled, the landscape offers room for projection, room to move but also to recover natural forms and bring them back home – to take them inward.

To any nineteenth-century male, family was a crucial component of legitimate social identity. Childless and wifeless, Thoreau's worldly identity was somewhat lacking, and apart from the two years he spent living in a cabin on Walden Pond, and a season or two in the Emerson household while Emerson was in England, his experience of family life came only through his parents, with whom he lived most of his life. Twenty-five years is about the amount of time it takes to produce an adult. Thoreau, who religiously kept a journal for 25 years, takes his relationship to his journal as seriously as any family (adult) commitment.

My Nature Book

My younger efforts at diary-keeping were unconvincing, disingenuous. I hadn't found the diary faith or creed. Quite soon I was spending all my time reading and my diary was nothing more than a forlorn notebook where I kept a scattered list of Books Already Read. Diary writing was a form of alter ego on patrol. Tiresome. It made me feel guilty. Like maths, I couldn't really do it. Why keep a list of only some of the books you've read? Just read. Nobody was checking.

Reading took up all my time: the seven-minute walk to the town library where you could only borrow five books before the lady with the long sloping nose pulled down her glasses and started looking at you strangely. 'You've five already you know,' she said as she watched me try to sneak in a sixth.

'They're both short,' I said, knowing how feeble that sounded.

'They may be short, dear, but that's still six, not five. Now run along. That lot should keep you going for a few weeks.'

'I'll be done in a week,' I said in my quiet, steady, sounding-like-a-teacher voice. 'And then it's the weekend and you're only open half a day on Saturday. I have to do chores on Saturday.'

The lady's nose looked shiny and beaky like a bird's. She sniffed and her nose suddenly built a bridge. 'A real reader, aren't you?'

Why did adults always speak to children as though they were five; always five and nothing more? I took my books home and stored them under my bed so no one would tread on them. I put my hand under the bed and felt for my diary. It was cold and damp and full of dust. I pushed it away again guiltily. I felt for the soft plastic covers of my library books. They were reassuringly warm.

The books I took home with me were always stories about creatures living in secret places: grey-bearded dwarves, grey-tailed rabbits, talking badgers and Borrowers. I preferred books to be about creatures, creatures who lived among forests and flowers and ate nettle soup for lunch. Creatures who went out rowing in boats. I wanted to be part of these secret, magical worlds, full of dandelions and ferns and fairy tale; worlds where flowers grew everywhere.

So for my birthday I asked for a flower press because my grandmother had told me that Victorian ladies pressed flowers and it sounded magical; pressing flowers was a 'lovely hobby', my grandmother said, and I could learn about nature that way. I could go out into the forests and fields and find rare specimens and bring them back home to examine and record. I could become a flower expert and keep their names stored away in my diary. My grandmother would teach me their names in Latin and I could learn to cast spells. I would chant their names out loud to myself at night. Instead of counting sheep I would recite Latin flowers.

When my flower press arrived I thought it looked like a wooden book. It was a wooden square standing on stilts with a shiny screw attached to each corner. I opened and closed the screws and they creaked. My flower press was a ladies' torture chamber filled with delicate leaves of dark and pale blue blotting paper.

'To keep everything nice and dry, airtight ... snug,' said my grandmother. 'Now be sure to keep it somewhere dry and warm.'

My flower press was an experiment and I was a scientist in a laboratory. I would need special gloves. I was going to collect specimens and record them; I was going to turn flowers into spells. This was my secret ritual, my peculiar habit. Pressing flowers was how I would know how long it took for something living to die.

So I went to Lobs Wood in search of special flowers. I found blue and white ones and I picked bags full. 'Bluebells and cow-parsley,' my grandmother said about the delicate creatures I took home, my drooping, fainting friends.

'Will they last?' I asked. 'The white ones keep losing their heads.'

'Spread them out nicely, dear, one on each page, and make a note of which you put in when. Keep a count of the days.'

Days? How long do they need to be in there for? I wanted my flowers to come out looking as pretty as the illustrations in my books; like the delicate drawings in the book about Grey-Dwarves living on the Bright Stream. How long did it take to kill and keep a flower?

'You'll need to give it a week, dear, at least.'

A week? That was as long as it would take to read all my

books. So I sat on the floor of my room reading with my flower press against my side, holding it under my arm, twisting its silver screws and turning it around and around. I liked to feel it dig into my side. Every day I opened it; then twice a day, then more. I couldn't stop opening it to check on my dead friends. Were they still alive; had they changed colour? Were they stuck to the leaves?

Now I think of it my flower press was another form of diary-keeping. I was counting time passing: mornings and afternoons, two or three hours, parcels of time between lunch and dinner, between doing my chores. I was waiting for something to happen because nothing ever did, except in books. But something would come out of this book, something magically transformed. I was a sorceress creating her spells. This was my Eleusinian mystery, my secret rite, my peculiar habit, the thing I did when no one was looking. This was how I felt Important, like Pooh Bear. I knew things no one else did. No one but me could tell what exactly was happening inside my flower press. It was better than a diary because I didn't have to make up Very Exciting Things. And at the end, after I'd counted down enough days, I had something I could pull out from it: a flower pressed as thin as a wafer, delicate blue tissue paper. Bluebells took about a week. Cow-parsley took longer because it had wild hair standing on end: ten days, sometimes two weeks, ten books later.

Natural Time

All diaries invest in some form of narrative cycle, stories that tell the passing of time. Thoreau's preferred sense of time is ancient. Trees, plants, Indian arrowheads – the gathering of which constituted one of the 'regular pursuits of spring' – evoke an American prehistory, an ancient temporality Thoreau would like to track down on his long nature walks. He tells his journal:

> the Indian arrowhead will balk [Time's] efforts and Eternity will have to come to his aid ... I would fain know that I am on the trail of the mind ... When I see these signs I know that the subtle spirits that made them are not far off ...[102]

In Thoreau's journal, 'time' is quite literally stored up, as page after page of the word and its associations circulate through the leather-bound volumes. Time as lived experience converts into 'moments' or 'hours', small intervals of time passing, all wafting towards eternity. Time, like the particular aspects of the natural world, is a rare commodity. It is worth noting. Natural time, according to Thoreau, is superior to all forms of temporality precisely because it is bountiful; it is truly economical because it is always well spent: 'Nature has never lost a day, nor a moment ... In the moment, in the aeon, well employed, time ever advances with this rapidity ... The plant that waited a whole year, and then blossomed the instant it was ready and the earth was ready for it ... was rapid.'[103] Nature, in other words, handles time with conscience. It does so because its purpose is clear: it knows when and what to do in an instant.

*

On the other side of the Atlantic, Thoreau's English contemporary, fellow naturalist Reverend Francis Kilvert, was filling
his personal pages with news from the natural world. In
Kilvert's diary, landscape and community are firmly allied. His
version of nature shares more with society than Thoreau's, and
nature is often brought to him through social events or against
a backdrop of human activity. His view of the world comes,
as Thoreau's does, from a great deal of walking. Kilvert's diary
is evidence of a person in motion. Stylistically, this produces
a flecked, mobile and mutable sort of writing – quick and light
of foot – reflective of the species of plant and wildlife he
passes by. But in contrast to Thoreau, there is a major addition
to the range of species: the human.

Kilvert begins his diary where Thoreau leaves off. Ten years
after the American naturalist has ceased his journal entries,
Kilvert, in early 1870, is beginning his record of picaresque
rural life in Radnorshire, on the Welsh border. Here is a typical entry from the winter of the diary's nativity, Wednesday,
February 9th 1870:

> A very cold night and a slight shower of snow fell early
> this morning … Went up the Cwm to White Ash. Old
> Sarah Probert groaning and roll-ing about in bed. Read
> to her Mark vi and made sure she knew the Lord's Prayer
> by heart, making her repeat it. Hannah Jones smoking a
> short black pipe by the fire, and her daughter, a young
> mother with dark eyes and her hair hanging loose, nurs-
> ing her baby and displaying her charms liberally. Went
> with the Venables to dine at Whitney Court, driving in
> the mail phaeton and sitting behind with Charlie. Bitterly
> cold with a keen E. wind but we were well wrapped up

and the hood kept the wind off us going. Miss Jane from the Rectory at dinner … The Squire and his mother made the rest of the party. A grand night with stars glittering frosty keen and we came home at a rattling pace.[104]

Though this is not a travel journal, the entry has a terrific pace to it. Kilvert is a roamer; he is a man who moves across the depth and breadth of his community. Many forms of life are accounted for, from the grand, impassive gestures of the Welsh mountains and climate, to the breasts of Hannah Jones's daughter, to the night stars: all are part of the look of the universe. In between there is the smallness of the community he tends to, snugly enclosed between morning and night skies. Kilvert has a definite place in this world: not just as parish minister, but as community go-between. Nature, he observes, comes in many forms. The entry tells of a quiet faith in the sublime; God exists because there are the Welsh mountains covered in snow, a clear night sky, an order of serenity. Still, the human experience never leaves the scene. The carriage journey home from Whitney Court is remembered for its 'rattling pace'. Kilvert's bones shook. They felt the cold. Human life is viewed as a series of roles played out: everyone has their part to play.

Kilvert's several pastoral roles include lending literature, calling upon the sick and ailing and admiring pretty girls. He admires girls much as he does a rare species of flora and fauna, reading them as an extension of the picturesque villages and homes that are their 'natural' setting:

Thursday, 29 June 1871
Villaging. I went to the Old Mill to see the beautiful child. A group of girls on their way home from market

loitered by the stile above the Old Mill, resting and chattering over the stile. The Old Mill was silent, deserted, locked. I left a leaf in the latch hole. The brook twinkled past the house. Two cows grazed in the orchard slope across the brook above the house, and the gate of the poor little garden leaned and tottered, a frail defence against a cow with proclivities for cabbage.[105]

The whole effect is tender and naïve, like a child's drawing. Daily life is counted in simple units: a single leaf in a door; two cows in a field, a few girls sitting upon a stile. There are no crowds, no sense of the multitude. One can find a pretty face and form and admire it. Kilvert bestows a great deal of affection upon the singularly pretty. His journal pictures are bright and shiny, well lit. There is something of the happy childhood in many of his entries; rays of sun stored up to read on dark winter nights.

Here is Easter Day, April 1870:

The happiest, brightest, most beautiful Easter I have ever spent. I woke early and looked out. As I had hoped the day was cloudless, a glorious morning. My first thought was 'Christ is Risen'. It is not well to lie in bed on Easter morning, indeed it is thought very unlucky… There was a heavy white dew with a touch of hoar frost on the meadows, and as I leaned over the wicket gate by the mill pond looking to see if there were any primroses in the banks but not liking to venture into the dripping grass suddenly I heard the cuckoo for the first time this year… I loitered up the lane again gathering primroses.[106]

This a man romancing nature alone. His deeds are small and

local, unheroic, but there is texture and taste to the experience. We can taste and touch the grassy bank, the dew, the soft turf, the primroses. Everything asks to be touched, like a scrapbook of pressed flowers. At this point, and indeed many others, Kilvert is closer to Adelaide Pountney's *Diary of a Victorian Lady*, whose nature walks were recorded and accompanied by delicate specimens of flower. In the role of spring maiden, Kilvert traipses through the flower-filled meadow. We imagine him putting flowers in his hair.

Painting words and pictures

Kilvert is as entranced by the beauty of the natural world as he is by young girls; he is as heady with sensation as any teenage girl. Water and wind combine with light and shade to produce nature's special effects. The crucial words here are 'more' and 'completely', a language of pure desire:

> *Saturday 26th July 1873*
> At the bottom of the hill in the sunny hollow where we crossed a little stream of limpid water clear as crystal, dazzling and gleaming over its yellow pebbles, we met a woman who in answer to my companion's enquiries directed him to the sheepwashing. And presently we came to the gate of the meadow where the rural festival was being held. A group of men whose clothes were splashed and dyed by the red wash were plunging sheep and lambs one by one into a long deep trough. The sheep went in white and came out red, protected by their dipping against the attentions of the fly, and walked away across the

meadow to join the nock, shaking the red wash in showers from their close-shorn fleeces.

The lane grew more and still more lovely. The morning
sunlight slanted richly across the road between the trees,
or struck here and there through a break in the foliage
and tipped a frond of fern with brilliant green light.
Broad alternate bars of sunshine and shadow sky across
the lane, the sunlight shone on the polished grey silvery
stems of a row of beeches, and a tender morning mist
hung dreamily over the wooded hollow of the dingle
below the road. The lane opened up into a high open
common across which the morning breeze from the sea
stirred freshly with a cool light after the warm shelter of
the hollow lanes. Beyond the common a gate let into a
shady road cool and damp, dark and quiet as a cloister. It
was completely overhung by trees, and the air was filled
with the fragant aromatic scent of the fir trees and the
soft carpet of fir needles with which the ground was
thickly strewn. The fields of ripening wheat began to glow
golden along the slopes of the blue hills and the ferns,
fresh washed by the rain of the night, beamed clear and
brilliant green where the sun slanted silently through the
windows of the wood.[107]

We are reminded of John Constable's painted rural landscapes
and the cosy prose miniatures of Thomas Hardy in which
characters nestle intimately among trees and hedgerows.
Kilvert is painting his local community, adding layer upon
layer of alliterative and assonant sound and colour: 'sea stirred',
'cool light', 'glow golden', 'slanted light', 'ferns fresh' and
'washed', 'hollow lanes', 'windows of the wood'. We are all eyes
and ears, stopping upon every phrase to peek and peer. Our

senses are agog. His lush and light-filled language recalls the language of his contemporary, poet and priest, Gerard Manley Hopkins, for whom journals were a way of pinning down the world in words.

*

Kilvert's verbal compositions are not quite as radical as those of Hopkins, whose early diary, begun in 1863, aged nineteen, spins words around on the page as though they were revolving across his tongue. In Hopkins's journal we see the world from all sides; the world is turned through his mouth. What concerns Hopkins is the sensory implication of the word in the world as it becomes an object in the mind of the poet. We hear the words in flight through the air, whizzing and whirling about like sycamore leaves, ready to alight upon the thing itself.

An entry from September 1863 sees him testing the relationship between the sounds of words and their meaning. The passage begins with a rumination on the 'gr' sounds in 'grief' and 'gruff' and then, 'crack, creak, croak, crake, graculus, crackle'. Following on from this, Hopkins tries out 'Moonlight hanging or dropping on treetops like blue cobweb.' And then, 'Also the upper side of the little grotted waves turned to the sky have soft pale-coloured cobwebs on them, the under sides green.' Finally, 'Note that the beaded oar, dripping, powders or sows the smooth with dry silver drops.'[108] These are snatches and glimpses of the natural world; one imagines small droplets of words falling upon his tongue, as Hopkins, the supreme taster of words – Hopkins the poet – searches for the most pleasing palette (and palate) of sounds.

*

There is Hopkins the poet, but there is also Hopkins the naturalist who would pin trees down to their botanical formation: the look of an oak leaf. But there is more at stake than simple observation of a genus. Hopkins is also cultivating images that can best represent how the mind sees things. His work is a form of poetic phenomenology; he wants his poetry to express how the mind receives and processes the image of a leaf; how it converts the leaf into sensory data. It is hard graft. Oak leaves don't simply have alternate long and short shoots; the overall effect is that of 'looking like bright keys', as a July 1867 journal passage fastidiously notes.[109]

Hopkins's careful droplets of image-data are being stored up as evidence of how the natural world works in the presence of the mind, or how the mind works in the presence of nature. It is not all poetry: there is also information to be stored away, with the sense that seeing might lead to better knowing, as natural images meet with the hard and soft surfaces of language and create a new plastic form.

Hopkins is not interested in scientific nomenclatures. Hopkins, like Kilvert, wants a more personal relationship. Both men are more interested in perception than botanical or biological systems of knowledge.[110] The difference between them is that Hopkins is less interested in making sense of the day, only in making sense of what he sees. By 1870 he is labelling this 'inscape'; that is, the distinct form of things as they appear in their natural environment. His journal is an 'inscape' of life, which is to say life as it is broken up into daily patterns: various bumps and ridges, soft and hard spots, difficult and smooth parts.

Hopkins sees theology in nature, a kind of split form within natural things suggestive of a symbolic division. The oak leaf is part of the natural world but it is also part of a symbolic system. Hopkins's is a natural theology. What he notes is not passage into the Church, his religion, but the religious offices of nature. His emphasis is on the multifariousness of nature as it appears under a microscopic lens. Hopkins is captivated by pattern, the tessellated forms of nature. He is a botanist at heart, but a botanist who would find a divine pattern in the form of a leaf: 'This skeleton inscape of a spray-end of ash I broke at Wimbledon this summer is worth noticing for the suggested globe; it is leaf on the right and keys on the left.'[111] The entry includes a pencil drawing. It is as though the leaves themselves present a symbolic form that comments on the natural shape of the leaf, a symbol that shadows the world.

In between this system of forms and symbols, there are tiny slithers of the account of Hopkins's Catholic conversion, giving hints of the spirit of man in the world. But these wisps of self-reportage disappear into the ether: 'Cold. Resolved to be a religious'; and the rather comic entry written from Switzerland: 'Sunday, but no Catholics, I found, at Meyringen. The day fine.' And then 'To Stonyhurst to the seminary.'[112] Catholicism is very much an afterthought. There may have been no Catholics spotted in Meyringen but two months later, on September 24th 1870, Hopkins sees the Northern Lights for the first time and a serious piece of natural theology erupts from this:

First saw the Northern Lights. My eye was caught by beams of light and dark very like the crown of horny rays the sun makes behind a cloud. At first I thought of silvery cloud until I saw that these were luminous and did not dim the clearness of the stars in the Bear. They rose slightly radiating thrown out from the earthline. Then I saw soft pulses of light one after another rise and pass upwards arched in shape but waveringly and with the arch broken. They seemed to float, not following the warp of the sphere as falling stars look to do but free though concentrical with it. This busy working of nature wholly independent of the earth and seeming to go on in a strain of time not reckoned by our reckoning of days and years but simpler and as if correcting the preoccupation of the world by being preoccupied with and appealing to and dated to the day of judgment was like a witness to God and filled me with delightful fear.[113]

Hopkins delights in what he sees as proof of nature's capacity for independent existence; he is pleased to see the stars pursue their own temporal pattern and trajectory beyond the everyday world of the human. In Hopkins's mind, this brings an apt reassurance of a divine scheme of things. His entry is a carefully pressed and presented template of cosmic order, in which God is solely in charge of time.

Daily life barely features in Hopkins's journal world; what is more important is the relationship between natural particulars and the theologically large: the meaning of the word 'horn', which he spends some time dissecting, and then the appearance of that word-shape in the sky as he gazes at the Northern Lights. His journal pays attention only to those forms of life that exist independently of man-made schemes. We get no real sense of the life of the man – of Hopkins himself.

Mum's Garden Diary

Mum kept a list of English roses in her Beatrix Potter diary. When she bought it I thought that Mr Macgregor was now in charge of our garden.

On the front of her diary Mr Macgregor was waving his rake at Peter Rabbit; Peter Rabbit is running away as fast as he can from that pointy rake. Peter Rabbit has his blue waistcoat open and his bunny tummy is on full show. I always thought that was because he was gardening, or 'pottering' as Mum called it, which meant moving slowly up and down the garden path talking to the begonias and the roses. It meant walking about with a green tin watering can in your hand and sprinkling. When Mum was pottering in the garden you couldn't speak to her, not about anything. Not even about the roses.

Mum loved roses. She liked roses more than people. She was always talking about them. She'd drive out to the garden centre, off the dual carriageway, where she'd get herself a cup of coffee in peace and sit down and write out the names of old English roses. Roses had to smell nice, she said. That was their main job. It was no good having roses in your garden that didn't carry you off somewhere with their scent. Her list of names went something like this:

Penelope: pale pink, delicate scent, flowers late summer and early autumn. Hybrid musk. (By the rockery, along the wall.)

Madam Hardy: white, strong lemony fragrance, flowers early summer. Damask. (Near the apple tree. Ask Maisie to help me carry out the hose.)

Felicia: pink, very fragrant, flowers spring and autumn.

Hybrid musk. (Clear a space behind the dustbins. Move
the bikes, turn over the soil.)

Fantin Latour: powder pink, scented bush, mid-summer
flowering. Centifolia. (Ask the man whether the roots
will take to clay soil. How big will the bush grow?)

Mum's garden diary was trying to build something romantic
from a mess. When we moved in, our garden was rubble and
weeds, 'a council car park', she said. Mum dug it up and started
all over again. She bought a diary from Woolworths and started making notes on the best smelling roses in England. Her
diary was full of dates for planting and watering and pruning.

Roses need a lot of water, and in the summer of 1976 that
was a real problem. There was a ban on garden hoses, so Mum
had to go outside and cover her roses in white sheets to protect
them from the glare of the sun. My grandma said that was
taking things too far. What would the neighbours say? I said
that the neighbours already knew about us. It was too late, so
what did it matter.

Mum's roses were her ancient, feminine friends. I imagined
them as old ladies sitting around in a nursing home talking to
one another about their garden positions. Some of them would
be cross, dissatisfied, grumbling. 'What does she think she's
playing at planting me by the bins?' Felicia was not happy. Her
life had been ruined by the strong smell of rotting nappies.
'That is no prospect for a lady. It's ruining my scent.'

I didn't know what it meant to be a 'damask' or a 'musk' or a
'hybrid'. But I thought that must mean the colour and texture
of their petals, the kind of dresses they wore. But in my mum's
diary they were still young ladies. Her diary was where she
arranged dances for her roses, like they did in Jane Austen.
'On May 31st Miss Felicia will go to the Ball at (what was that

place called where Mr Darcy lived ... Or was it Mr Bingley?)
Netherfield Grange!'

I wrote it out in my diary: 'Miss Felicia Musk is cordially
invited to dance with Mr Bingley at Netherfield Grange.
Parasols will be provided.'

'Roses need plenty of sun and shade,' said Mum. 'It's always
a delicate dance. Now, Sally, go and get that nice bit of soil
from the bottom of the apple tree. I've been saving it to cover
the roots of my Felicia. She doesn't look very happy at the
moment, does she?'

*

Diaries can carry a lot of petty detail. But not all diarists
choose to write about themselves or others. Details can per-
tain to other things.

Self is certainly not the subject for George Orwell, whose
gnomic domestic diaries tell very little of the man himself.
What they do divulge is a great deal of detail about what
grows in his garden: his beloved green space in Wallington,
Hertfordshire.

Beginning his diary in the spring of 1939, Orwell keeps a
'domestic' diary, close to the genre of the species-spotting
Victorian naturalist. The effect, for the reader, is peculiar; here
is Orwell at his most individual, you might say, his most odd.
He has no intention of writing autobiography or memoir.
This is not life history but the jottings of a man whose focus is
narrow and eccentric:

August 11, 1938
This morning all surfaces, even indoors, damp as a result
of mist. A curious deposit all over my snuff-box, evident-

ly residue of moisture acting on lacquer. Very hot, but rain in the afternoon.

Am told the men caught another snake this morning – definitely a grass snake this time. The man who saw them said they had tied a string round its neck & were trying to cut out its tongue with a knife, the idea being that after this it could not 'sting'.

The first Beauty of Bath apples today. [114]

Here is a radically apolitical Orwell, an Orwell stripped of rhetoric and metaphor, a man talking only to himself. This is a man in pottering mode; there is no argument and barely a sense of place. And his is a jumpy mind, a mind that trails off from one subject to another: from mist to snakes and a brief tale of a local man who cut the sting from a grass snake – and then, finally, apples.

The effect is fabulous and ever so slightly absurd in its biblical resonances. The mention of apples comes as a relief in the final line; here is something recognisably domestic. But Orwell's domestic diaries are definitely potty and pottering. There is little sense of the outside world, the larger orders of time and space. Mostly he writes of his garden: what is budding or 'berrying'; what is pushing up through the soil. Time and place are only known at all by the date and place noted at the top of the entry, the only clue we have to his back-and-forth movements between Hertfordshire and his parents' house in Southwold, Kent. It is often hard to work out where Orwell is:

August 22
Warmish day, with showers. Nights are getting colder & more like autumn. A few oaks beginning to yellow very

slightly. After the rain enormous slugs crawling about, one measuring about 3" long. Large holes, presumably ear-holes, some distance behind head. They were of two distinct colours, some light fawn & others white, but both have a band of bright orange round the edge of the belly, which makes one think they are of the same species & vary individually in colour. On the tip of their tails they had blobs of gelatinous stuff like the casing of water-snail's eggs.[115]

Reading Orwell we find ourselves nuzzled up close to slugs. We're reminded of Woolf lying close to the ground around Asheham with her caterpillar. She, nonetheless, is still looking for narrative – the journey of a butterfly emerging from its chrysalis. Orwell is merely looking for signs of life.

Orwell's is a myopic view of natural life, such that the heads and tails of slugs take up the whole, magnifying lens. We only know where we are, where Orwell is, by gathering together other scraps of information. Beneath this entry sits a newspaper cutting on how to make sloe gin. The entry before it includes a pencil drawing of the ancient grave mound on Blue Bell Hill, Aylesford, Kent, locally called Kit's Coty House, and what Orwell calls a 'druidical altar of some kind'. Doodles and drawings make much of this diary a sort of scrapbook of local information, in which the particular site of the locale often remains rather blurry.

Time and place are scattered across eccentric arrangements of information: a summary of the day's weather, the size of the ear holes of slugs and the shape of a druidical grave. Orwell is a man who likes gathering bits of unrelated information; his diaries often read like some sort of strange and uninterpreted diagram. Unlike Hopkins, he refuses any grand scheme of things.

Orwell's scattered domestic world is kept quite separate from his world of politics, war, social observation and travel. His earlier diary, begun on the last day of January 1936, is an account of his road to the Wigan Pier project, the work that became published as *The Road To Wigan Pier* (1937) – a study of the 'distressed areas' of northern England. Orwell's Wigan Pier in part emerged from a diary dedicated to the experience, and, unlike his domestic diaries, it has a story to tell. There is a narrative partly because there is a journey, but also because there is a real social purpose. Orwell's Wigan diary, like his later war diary, is a piece of social journalism. His so-called domestic diary is a series of 'spottings' of buds, shoots, berries and leaves; of the number of eggs laid by his chickens (there is something very serious about this system of account); and a series of jottings on the weather. Like Woolf in Asheham, and other weather diarists, Orwell almost always begins his domestic diary with an account of the skies.

Orwell's lack of domestic narration is also partly explained by his perpetual migrancy. Wallington, although a home for ten years, was only so intermittently; Orwell went to Spain during the Civil War (1936–7), to Morocco from September 1938 to March 1939, to London during the war years, and then, finally, to Jura in 1946 after the death of his wife, Eileen. In addition, he continued to make regular visits to his parents' home. In and around the small-scale business of the domestic diary, where nothing is going on except apples and strawberries ripening, is the much larger business of war. But war is an entirely separate business from domestic pottering and asks for a grander rhetoric, a narrative and, more importantly, opinion.

Peter Davison's recent collection for Penguin has 'intercalated', the war diaries with the domestic. What we get is an awkward narrative of 'Events Leading Up to the War', in which the domestic diary is interrupted by a list of newspaper extracts reciting the facts of German mobilisation. The effect is a clever comment on the uninterrupted blitheness of daily rural England, where the only thing that still counts is the rain. But the end of the diary breaks into something more like political commentary: suddenly, Orwell the journalist emerges, providing a summary of the state of the nation as it appears inside and outside print – England in the news and the England that goes unrecorded – alongside the recent implementation of the Military Training Act. Writing from Greenwich in early September 1939, he summarises the mood of London: 'No panic, on the other hand, no enthusiasm, & in fact not much interest.'[116]

Domestic life is under the constant threat of mobilisation – not only from Orwell's own to-ing and fro-ing but also from the more radical dislocation of war. Against the backdrop of the imploding political world, the docile world of the back garden is a paradise of the inconsequential, the completely non-eventful. On the last day of August 1939, three years after Orwell began his domestic diary, he completes two separate diary entries. The first records his habitual form of life on the home front (he writes from Hampshire, but the entry is as uniform as those he writes from Wallington): 'Hot, yesterday & today fairly heavy rain. Blackberries are ripening in this district. Finches beginning to flock. Very heavy mists in the early morning.'[117] The fact is that Orwell's version of rural England is much the same wherever he is; rural Hertfordshire and rural Hampshire both have mist and seasons of mellow fruitfulness, berries ripening in the harvest sun. Domesticity is blissfully samey and nature-spotting a reassuring habit.

The second entry, on the following day, blasts through this quiet contentment. It is a declaration of war: 'Invasion of

Poland began this morning. Warsaw bombed. General mobilisation proclaimed in England, ditto in France plus martial
law. [Radio].'[118] Sleepy rural England is under threat and
Europe is in a state of crisis. Domestic life is rendered trivial
in the face of 'events leading up to war'. Orwell has been
listening to his radio, as he was to do throughout the duration
of the war.

Despite this radical interruption, Orwell continues with his
domestic diary: from September 5th 1939 to the end of April
1940 – eight more months of comments on the weather and
the state of the soil. These are his private passions. Reading
these entries one becomes aware that his reports from the
garden constitute a daily mantra against the changeable
nature of his domestic arrangements and the even larger
turmoil of the public world. For a man as politically involved
as Orwell, a samey report from the garden is a source of
comfort in the face of the precarious reports coming in from
the public world. Life in the garden continues, for now. The
hens are still laying.

CHAPTER FOUR

GOING PUBLIC

Orwell chooses to keep his domestic interests and the life of the world quite separate, his garden from his war. Diaries can negotiate the often difficult gap between private and public persona, our front from our back door self. The line between the two is often frail and shifting. Sometimes that line can completely disappear. Our diary is a reminder of our public-private split etiquette, our two very different faces.

Front Door and Back Door Faces

There was nowhere very private in the house I grew up in. Even the loo wasn't private because the door was always broken. 'That catch has gone again,' said my grandmother. 'What a nuisance. Well, we'll all just have to be especially careful and polite and knock before we go in.' Of course no one ever did.

Likewise our bathroom was a draughty waiting room, a place where moss and lichen pushed rudely in through the window. Private activities were definitely off-limits. You didn't linger in our bathroom; you dipped in and dipped out, thinking yourself lucky if you were only number two in the bath-water queue. Privacy hadn't much currency at 14 Granville Road, Littlehampton, West Sussex. You had to go outside for that.

For my mother, that meant putting on her Front Door Face. Mum had two faces: for half the week she was the woman with pale, wan looks, her hair wrapped up inside curlers beneath a dirty blue scarf. Half of the week my mum was a woman still arranging herself. For the other half she was the Duchess of Devonshire or a member of the House of Windsor, a woman with hay-stacked golden hair soaring skywards, propped up by half a can of L'Oréal hairspray and several vicious metallic pins. Mum was good at looking elevated. When she had her Front Door Face on she meant business. Public and private were mutually exclusive categories in my childhood home; much of it had to do with hair.

Mrs Sturgess next door used to say that Mum looked like the PM going out to get her lunch. I thought that was a stupid comment because Margaret Thatcher would never have to go and get her own lunch. 'Such a nice outfit she puts together,' Mrs Sturgess said to me when I went outside to put out the rubbish. 'Your mum looks like a real aristo … You can't miss her, can you?' I thought this rather rude.

Mum never went anywhere without her handbag: 'Where on earth is my bag? Which one of you swines has hidden it?' she would cry as she lurched along the hallway, reaching for the door. Her handbag was her artillery store, the repository for her huge lump of keys and her precious date diary. Her diary was an integral part of her wardrobe. Over the years its looks changed from a silver-gold patent affair to an Edwardian Lady's Diary in miniature: a delicate nose-spray of paper and shiny plastic that sat at the bottom of her brassy black handbag waiting to spring to life. On the back page of her diary Mum kept 'all her numbers'.

'All her numbers' was how Mum accessed the world. We were never allowed to touch or tamper with that list. Here, in a small, carefully copied, tightly pressed script my mother kept a list of telephone numbers, her code in the world: the number of Bentalls, the department store in Worthing (with a direct line to the perfume counter); Coopers, the greengrocer's round the corner where she added every day or so to the enormous grocery list; Pegrums, the baker's, the Cake Shop in the Arcade, the bank manager at Barclays who was 'always delighted to hear from you, Mrs Bayley'; Oxendens, the hardware shop where she would send us to pick up light bulbs, 'the last of those lovely soft-pink ones you've had in store for a while ... I do hope you have them still. It would be very silly of you to have got rid of them ... you know how often they blow ...'

My mother's date diary was where our network of errands began. From there, she summoned the pounds and pounds of minced meat we carried back from Dewhurst, the butcher's; the 10 or 12 pounds of Extra Sharp Canadian Cheddar that came with it (which shamefully required a lady's shopping trolley to pull back). 'Not quite so sharp this week,' she'd say on the phone, her diary open at the crease, its small, firmly focused bookmark running down the centre matching the lines across the forehead. 'Not quite as sharp as I like. I do hope you're not letting your standards slip. It is meant to be "Extra Sharp Canadian" after all ... and we do come to you because you have the best cheddar ... I wouldn't want to have to cancel our regular order ...'

Years later I realised that, in a household made up of women, my mother was the only one among us who knew how to draw out of the world what we needed; to trade, barter and banter with the petty businessmen who held the key to our week's lunches and dinners. Mum knew how to use 'all her numbers' to draw in an entire battery of goods: toilet roll, light bulbs, cheese, Weetabix, 20 pints of milk, 10 packets of butter, 8 pounds of minced meat, a large farmhouse loaf, a set of raffle tickets from the school, a free sample of Oil of Ulay with her Bentalls card. When she pulled out her diary and got on the phone she meant business. When she left the house with her hair on stilts, she meant it even more. 'All her numbers' negotiated the overdraft that meant one Christmas we could still afford Brussels sprouts and stuffing; all her numbers plus her hair.

*

Long before Virginia Woolf, Samuel Pepys was chronicling London life, the city's crowds and its folkish pageantry. Certainly he was writing if not making history, and consequently his diary is a rich store of seventeenth-century life. In the England of the 1660s, public and private spheres are not yet clearly defined and differentiated realms of experience. Pepys's interest in the world of politics and international events arises from his position as a high-level naval administrator. Naturally, he was interested in the unfolding saga of the Dutch Wars, the most intriguing international situation of his lifetime. It was his professional business to know how to handle the slim budget assigned to the navy at the outbreak of the Second Anglo-Dutch War in 1665. His diary affords him something more luxurious: a place for airing his private political thoughts and opinions such that, at the end of the war in 1667, Pepys can muse upon the superiority of the Dutch people and the negligence of King Charles in not looking 'after his business'.[119]

Pepys was a great follower of public affairs and an avid reader of newspapers. His library, now housed at Magdalene College, Cambridge, confirms this. Among other records, Pepys kept a forty-year sequence of the bi-weekly *London Gazette*. As a civil servant swiftly rising in rank, knowledge of the public world was essential to advancement in his career. His diary is stuffed with references to the 'public', a term that might be considered loosely synonymous with Pepys's take on political affairs, particularly those surrounding the monarchy, and his commitment as civic administrator to the work of the state. As his career begins to take off, he becomes an avid gatherer of political news – often hurrying off to Westminster Hall or Miles's coffee house on the Embankment to catch the latest drift of opinion.[120] Above all, he is a serious watcher of the royals.

'Coronacion Day' April 1661 is a big day for Pepys. As clerk to the Earl of Sandwich – Sandwich since 1659 a staunch royalist and senior official in the navy – we find Pepys up at 4am helping to prepare Westminster Abbey. His night has been spent sharing a bed with a certain Mr Sheply, steward to the earl. We might think of this as an intimate start, but the truth is that Pepys's workaday world is far more feudal than we might imagine. The divisions of the modern world created by money and rank are still emerging in seventeenth-century London. Pepys might well share a bed with a steward just as he might eat, sleep and frolic among the servants of the earl's household. He does both. Roaming between high and low, Pepys maintained the habits of an earlier feudal culture in which access to the servants might include, if he was lucky, sexual favours from the earl's housekeeper. Later that same day, he might also enjoy the privilege of dining with the earl's wife – if her husband was absent on business: both were perfectly manageable in one day.[121]

Pepys is a proud and excited participant in public affairs; on Coronation Day, he is one of the crowds but also keen to attach himself to men of rank. His record of the event is a superb piece of historical journalism. Above all, it tells a story of rank beginning and ending on high. Perched high upon scaffolding, Pepys looks down with a bird's-eye view upon the royal parade. What interests him is the ceremonial order of things: the props and proceedings of this display. When his view of the coronation is blocked, Pepys joins in with the dismayed crowds: 'And then in the Quire at the very high altar he passed all the ceremonies of the Coronacion – which, to my very great grief, I and most in the Abbey could not see.'[122]

His style is much in the mode of a modern-day television broadcast. His shots are broad and panoramic; everything must be accounted for, nothing missed out. He writes as a man on the ground reaching for the men in the air. Rank impresses him, as do the ceremonial arts of the royal show. Pepys takes pleasure in seeing the Duke of York, a man with whom, in the course of time and through professional advancement, he will be more closely associated. He revels in the sight of his 'Lord' carrying the King's sceptre. He is tremendously pleased when the King and the Duke of York, the King's brother, notice him among the crowds. Nothing delights him more. All at once he is part of the glamour and the glitter, the overwhelming show of gold and silver, so much he can barely take it in.

Pepys's account of the coronation is a spectacular piece of visual recall worthy of a public broadcast. He is the royal reporter on the ground:

And a pleasure it was to see the Abbey raised in the middle, all covered with read and a throne (that is a chaire) and footstool on the top of it. And all the officers of all kinds, so much as the very fidlers, in red vests. At last comes in the Deane and prebends of Westminster with the Bishops (many of them in cloth-of-gold Copes; and after them the nobility in all their parliament robes, which was a most magnificent sight). Then the Duke and the King with a scepter (carried by my Lord of Sandwich) and Sword and mond before him, and the crowne too. The King in his robes, bare-headed, which was very fine.[123]

Confidently pro-monarchy, Pepys's report is the seventeenth-century equivalent of the recent global television phenomenon that was the British royal wedding; there is the same sense of everyone being there, whether lining the streets between Buckingham Palace and Westminster Abbey, or at home, glued to the screen. Pepys is craning his neck as much as anyone. The difference is that he writes as a close bystander, peering into the proceedings as though he has some right to be included. To be precise, Pepys is a royal hanger-on. He would like to think of himself as part of the royal household and, in due course, he comes close to being one.

It is worth considering what it is Pepys achieves in his diary. This distinctly personal document at once records intensely private experiences – affairs with his servants, rows with his wife – alongside national history. But in Pepys's late seventeenth-century London, there are fewer fixed categories for daily experience. Historically speaking, Pepys lags just behind what sociologist Jurgen Habermas has described as the emergence of a public sphere: an eighteenth-century phenomenon involving the use of public space – namely coffee houses and taverns – for discussion of public life.[124]

Public life, in other words, is made up of discourse, chat. Of course, Pepys is already doing this. He is also doing what we all do in public: talk about others, gossip and trade tittle-tattle. What we now think of as the public sphere, of which political debate is an aspect, rose partly from an emerging newspaper culture, political pamphlets and broadsides. The Elizabethans invented these and the Stuarts continued to distribute them. Suddenly, there was a place to say something publicly.[125] But the public sphere was not simply a place to shout about politics. With the rise of a market economy, the realm of the family became dependent upon the marketplace.[126]

Of course there is a great deal of difference, but not in Pepys's writing up of the two experiences. Both constitute news of the day, and in the public spaces of Stuart England news came by word of mouth. Certainly in Pepys's world there is a thriving public sphere: a place between civil society and the state in which matters of interest to private individuals – family matters, politics and matters of personal fortune – are all discussed.[128] News really is the word on the street and a great deal of Pepys's day seems to be taken up with 'discourse'.

Walking and talking are at the heart of Pepys's business world. It is by walking the streets that Pepys receives his news:

So, doing several things by the way, I walked home; and after dinner to the office all the afternoon. At night all the bells in the towne rung, and bonfires made for the joy of the Queenes arrivall … But I do not see much thorough joy, but only an indifferent one, in the hearts of people, who are much discontented at the pride and luxury of the Court, and running in debt.[129]

84

Pepys has a capacious civic imagination. From matters related to his professional status and office work, he turns to the sounds of the city – the church bells pealing out for the arrival of Catherine of Braganza from Portugal, Charles's new Queen. Suddenly, local London achieves a much larger vista: one that includes international relations as well as the attitudes of the populace to court politics. Public attitudes travel by and through the streets of London, and, as a man of the streets, Pepys picks up the medley of popular opinion 'by the way'.[130]

Pepys's diary consistently provides yearly accounts: first he gives a summary of his fiscal estate and then a summary of the state of the nation. In these two estates there is plenty of 'wonder' and 'mischief'. Pepys has his own vices, habits of 'negligence and prodigality', but he reviews them in relation to those of the state. The logic might be that if the state is misbehaving then Pepys's wayward behaviour, in comparison, seems a little less bad. The parallel works because in Pepys's London there are smaller distances between civic life and the world of Whitehall, Westminster Hall and the Royal Exchange. As Pepys moves up in the public world, Charles and his entourage become more and more present; accordingly, their fortune seems as much to determine Pepys's mood as his life at home.

*

All the talking in my home came straight from my aunt's favourite television programmes, *Spitting Image*, *EastEnders* and *Murder She Wrote*. My mum was called Angela and so was the lady who ran the pub on *EastEnders*; and then so, I realised, was the detective in *Murder She Wrote*. They all liked talking. By talking, I mean what my mum called 'holding forth', what Angie in *EastEnders* called 'argie-bargie'. When my aunt got going with one of her rants, which is what my brother called them, we were all blown off course.

'That man has got something coming to him ... all that talk of trade unions and workers' rights ... wet, that's what it is, limp and leftie ... I mean look at him, Ange, he can't even do his anorak up properly ... he's standing there on a windy hill in Barnsley ... Barnsley isn't it ... and he can't even do his anorak up ... Wet, that's what it is. Wet! And you might have thought he'd put a comb through his hair ... this is his moment ... and look at him! He must have known the press were coming ... it can't have come out of nowhere, could it, Ange? I expect it's all part of the act ... make yourself look like someone who can't afford three shredded wheat in the morning and you'll have everyone feeling sorry for you. If any of you lot go out of the house looking like that you'll have it coming to you. He looks like he's just been dragged through the local Comp corridor ... by the scruff of his neck. We're all supposed to feel sorry for that man, that's what he wants ... he wants our pity. Well, he's not going to get it from me, Ange ... he's getting nothing like that from me!'

My mother nodded; my grandmother nodded. When my aunt got going all you could do was keep nodding.

Summing up History

Diaries negotiate the thin membrane between private and public lives, private and public history; a place where one form of history washes back and forth across the other. But diaries are intensely filtered documents; they channel history through the diarist such that he or she stands somewhere close to the centre. In its first incarnation the diary is not a public document; and yet the responsible diarist, particularly one in the public sphere, invariably writes with a wary eye on the future. Posthumous publication is always possible.

Pepys's diary practice is one that perpetually keeps an eye on posterity, a mind-set that informs the content and aesthetic of his diary. Summaries are commonplace, summaries of his own fortune alongside 'the state of the nation'. At the end of 1666 Pepys is again totting up his accounts:

> Myself and my family well, having four maids and one clerk, Tom in my house ... Our healths are well; only my eyes with overworking them ... Public matters in a most sad condition. Seaman discouraged for a want of pay... Our enemies, French and Dutch, great and grow more, by our poverty. The Parliament backward in raising, because jealous of the spending of the money. The city less and less likely to be built again, everybody settling elsewhere, and nobody encouraged to trade. A sad, vicious, negligent Court, and all sober men there fearful of the ruin of the whole Kingdom this next year – from which, good God deliver us. One thing I reckon remarkable in my own condition is that I am come to abound in good plate, so as at all entertainments to be served wholly with silver plates, having two dozen and a half.[131]

Pepys's annual accounts are comically subjective. The Puritan father in him frowns upon the prodigal condition of the court. But on matters personal – his rise in fortune and status – he is self-congratulatory and even smug. Pepys and his household are quite obviously in good 'condition' because he dines regularly from silver plates.

Government and the business of Parliament are constant matters in Pepys's world, and a walk up to Whitehall often opens his day. His business is almost always naval accounts: matters related to the Treasury. By 1665, his most frequent trip is to the Treasury Chamber where he discusses funds available for 'victualling': the naval provisions budget. Pepys's job at Whitehall is to extract as much money for the navy as possible. Going before the Treasury, he takes with him a carefully rehearsed piece of rhetoric and a convincing set of business accounts. This is his 'fair discourse of the Administracion of the Navy' to set before the King and his council; it is his 'bid'.[132]

Pepys is not just a good accountant; he is also a wily politician. He knows what side his bread is buttered on and spends as much time preparing his 'discourse' as he does winning friends and influence. The day before his day in council, he visits the Duke of York, the King's brother and the Lord High Admiral, in his chamber at Whitehall. Clearly a strategic move on Pepys's part, he receives sound and subtle advice from the Duke to alter one small but vital part of his paper – the line, 'upon the Rupture between the late King and the Parliament' to 'the beginning of the late Rebellion'. The Duke's point is that it was by the 'Rebellion' – shorthand for the Civil War, Cromwell and the execution of Charles I – that the navy will reinforce its 'old good course' and translate itself into a 'Commission'.[133] History is thus tweaked and revised slightly in favour of the navy. This is good politics.

Pepys's political savvy is on the rise and he is beginning to consider himself something of a 'Parliament man'. Having brandished his rhetorical talents on several occasions in

Parliament Hall, and built what he describes as a bit of a reputation for fine 'discourse', Pepys has developed several of the skills of the successful politician. Furthermore, he is now moving among the King's circle.[134] It is hardly surprising that he has begun to fancy himself as a political player.

But what makes Pepys credible as a politician is his committed attention to recorded history. Apart from his attempts at writing and gathering 'collections' of naval history,[135] Pepys was an assiduous keeper of lists and accounts: memorandum books, petty cash-books, letter-books, even a book of vows.[136] Historical recall, surely above all else, is vital for successful politicking and Pepys's diary, apart from his own professional attempts at naval history, is a fine piece of amateur history.

Pepys shows signs of understanding what philosopher Edmund Burke was later to espouse as a sort of moral historical consciousness, in which the present moment, in order to be understood better, ought to be read in the light of the accumulated wisdom of the past.[137] Pepys's diary lived through the Great Fire of London, the years of the Plague, and a war with the Dutch. As a document, it is one of the great records of seventeenth-century history. But it shouldn't be forgotten that Pepys's history is profoundly personal. Whatever his historical consciousness, it is always self-directed, read through the daily fluctuations in fortune of his home life: his relationship with his wife Elizabeth. You might say he and his diary are one of the great stock-takers of domestic life. It is also one of the great coming-of-age stories of public history.

At the same time, Pepys's diary is one of the few that reaches for some of the ambitions of the novel. Read across long runs of days, the diary produces a hero, and certainly a history. You could argue that Pepys's diary produces several histories, which might also be called plots. Often the diary tips towards the picaresque style of Fielding's *Tom Jones* or Defoe's *Moll Flanders*. It is full of local adventure and local heroes. Pepys is chief among them, as he launches himself upon his particular version of public history. In the history of the public world, who might be considered Pepys's inheritors?

*

Almost 100 years on from Pepys's stocktaking and story-telling, President-to-be and diarist, John Adams, is also launching himself upon the world. It is the spring of 1756, and as a young man of twenty-one and a school teacher in his first place of employment, he comes out into the world. He begins bolshily, imagining himself – as the young Sylvia Plath was to do in her journal 200 years on – playing at God. Fantasies overflow as he builds a world in miniature and at the centre places himself as soldier and statesman – his own version of Lilliput. Three feet high, his statesmen and generals are also virtuosos, potential members of the Royal Society. Entomologists and biologists, these are discerning men of science; as much in touch with their feelings as their mind. One could rely upon them to cry heartily as well as to erect monuments to great victories:

> I sometimes, in my sprightly moments, consider myself, in my great Chair at School, as some Dictator at the head of a commonwealth. In this little State I can discover all the great Genius's, all the surprizing actions and revolutions of the great World in miniature. I have severall renowned Generalls but 3 feet high, and several deep projecting Politicians in peticoats. I have others catching and dissecting Flies, accumulating remarkable pebbles,

cockle shells &c., with as ardent Curiosity as any Virtuoso in the royal society. Some rattle and Thunder out A, B, C, with as much Fire and impetuosity, as Alexander fought, and very often sit down and cry as heartily, upon being out spelt, as Cesar did ... In short my little school like the great World, is made up of Kings, Politicians, Divines, L.D ... Fops, Buffoons, Fidlers, Sychophants, Fools, Coxcombs, chimney sweepers, and every other Character drawn in History or seen in the World. Is it not then the highest Pleasure my Friend to preside in this little World?[138]

Like James Boswell, who preferred to practise his Saturday morning dialogue at Child's coffee house, the twenty-one-year-old Adams is rehearsing an ideal self. His miniature state is a kind of school or academy in which he plays both pupil and principal; he hasn't yet graduated but is already capable of imagining himself as a global leader. In truth, he wasn't far off. Although in his lifetime his influence was not as recognised as that of Jefferson or Washington, he is now remembered as one of the key contributors to the American Constitution.[139] What is most notable about this fantasy is the fact that Adams imagines himself as both young and old, with an identity stretching across epochs. Part fiction, part fantasy, Adams's entry is a sort of Game of Life in which he plays the role of school principal producing generations of future students. Which among them will turn out to be a fool and which a philosopher; are there, among them, any future heroes of state?

Diaries breed fantasies. With no one watching or listening, the diarist can imagine himself in all sorts of absurd postures and places. Adams's diary fluctuates between the more conventional form of a private journal and that of a commonplace book, where he muses upon philosophies and methods for living. Three years on from his imperial fantasy, he has begun to ask himself how he might best conduct business. Adams, by now, is a trained lawyer, newly appointed to the Bar. He has begun to think like a lawyer, to ask all the right questions. How does a successful man of the world operate? Certainly, he must go into the world, spend time in taverns, coffee houses and the town meeting house. Business cannot be done at home. Mix with all and sundry is Adams's advice to himself. Throw yourself among the crowds; join in with the local chit-chat. A man of business must be known. Save your reading for your leisure time.

Talking the Talk

Adams's philosophy is a pragmatic one. His diary is there as much to serve him in his public and business life as it is in his private affairs. It acts as useful witness for the defence or prosecution of public characters. Here, he can observe the effect of character upon character, note individual traits and reactions and learn to modify his approaches accordingly. He pays careful attention to his manners and gestures with the local dignitaries of his home town, Braintree, Massachusetts: 'Should always speak and shake Hands with the Deacon, inquire after his Wife, Sons, and humour his talkative Disposition.' Regarding 'Dr Savil and his Wife', Adams regrets having 'acted ... at Random' with them. He would do better to behave with more restraint around them, by 'visiting seldomer', using 'tender and soothing' language, accepting invitations to ride out with Mrs Savil and reading plays to them on occasional evenings, and thus he might win their influence.[140] On such occasions, Adams's diary takes on the role of etiquette book or a piece of social anthropology of local manners and customs. 'How to Win Friends and Influence People' – the subtle mechanisms of social engineering – this is his real training field.

As we have already determined, diaries are identity experiments; more specifically they are launching pads into the world. Adams's diary reminds us of the role of the diary as a training ground for future selves. Pepys, Boswell and Adams all share an urgent desire to contribute something to the public world. Their diaries often read as preparatory exercises to going public.

For Adams, social identity was developed by good conversation. Lively discourse should flow with as much force and ease as the Thames or Boston's Charles River. James Boswell was also quick to understand this: in order to be a man of the world, one had to master the art of conversation, smart anecdotes and, from there, witty reportage. Reading Adams and Boswell we are aware how much journals are also just forms of entertainment and self-amusement.

But conversation has to have a good subject and a hospitable venue. From Johnson, Boswell learned to regard the tavern as 'the throne of human felicity'. In the Mitre Tavern in London's Ely Court, Johnson met with Boswell for their first proper engagement on June 25th 1763. Boswell's public world is one largely built upon conversation. His version of public life is less formal than the future President's, more a matter of bonhomie and good show of character. Boswell wanted his journal to reflect well upon himself. He wanted a good write-up. His London Journal is written with some of the canny foresight of a novelist, often written with roughly a week's lag behind events.[141] For about a week, Boswell knows what will happen next. A week is sufficient time not to make a complete fool of yourself: it is enough time to plan ahead and practise what one might say and do.

In the modern world we might say that it is enough time to appear professional. While Boswell is not the public intellectual turned President that Adams is, he is not entirely amateur either. Adams understood that his journal might help make a man of him. He could take to his journal all the 'Intrigues, Acts, Passions, Speeches' of the public world.[142] Like Boswell, he is on the lookout for character and a good delivery. Among the community of Worcester, Massachusetts, he notes Parson Wiberts's 'popularity'; as a man of 'wit' and 'humour' he makes waves.[143] His familiar and easy style of conversation means people open up to him. For such a man, the transition between business and pleasure, public and private self, is barely perceptible.

CHAPTER FIVE

IN THE POLITICAL EYE

The House of Secret Scribblers

The house where I grew up was a den of secret scribblers. Everyone was at it, especially my aunt, who kept a secret notebook under her bed. We all knew it was there but none of us was allowed to go near it. My aunt's journal was protected by a force-field. We knew that if we went near it we'd be zapped.

My aunt kept a journal because she believed that what she had to say, what she knew, was extraordinary. She was storing up important secrets, as important as those Cardinal Wolsey went around with in the sixteenth century: Cardinal Wolsey was her hero. 'Wolsey' she called him as though he were her pet. 'Come, Wolsey, come … come here, Wolsey!' She pored over his picture in the book on Tudor history borrowed from the library. She traced the bulky shape of his outline. Late at night she whispered to him all the secrets she couldn't tell anyone else.

We studied Cardinal Wolsey at school. In the famous painting the cardinal is a bloated turkey; a mountain of flesh floating beneath a ballooning red gown. He clutches a roll of paper in his hand and lifts two fingers in front of him as though he were summoning servants. Cardinal Wolsey is always summoning someone, like my aunt is always summoning my grandmother. He is the most important person in the whole of England. When I look at his face I think it is smug and full of secrets, underneath those folds of soft pink paper for cheeks and a chin.

Cardinal Wolsey is the King's Lord Chancellor and he carries the Great Seal under his arm; inside that seal (which makes him the second only in the kingdom to Henry VIII) he carries all the gossip from the court back to his private chamber in his Very Large House at Hampton Court. There he scribbles in his journal all the negative thoughts he has on the marriage between King Henry and Anne Boleyn. He doesn't like Anne Boleyn but he has to keep that to himself. Anne Boleyn suspects that he is against her but Henry doesn't; not for a long time, not until it was too late.

Wolsey knows how to guard secrets. My aunt said Wolsey was an evil man but she liked him all the same because he had 'charisma', which meant he possessed an irresistible charm. His influence spread far and wide: at Whitehall and York Palace and Hampton Court and in Rome with the Pope and then at the Field of the Cloth of Gold, where he tried to improve relations between Henry and Francis, the King of France. Cardinal Wolsey charmed everybody with his fluently rehearsed French and his shower of gifts, until his devious machinations came to light, triggering his downfall.

*

In her journal my aunt was making history: our history. Over the years the journal turned into a scrapbook, then piles of photograph albums, then video tapes. One day she'd send it to the BBC and they would make a documentary about us. Everybody would comment on our strange clothes. Nobody would believe that 16 or 17 people lived in our small, stacked-up house.

When I was sent to Switzerland with my diary she was practising what Cardinal Wolsey had: statecraft, which sounds a bit like witchcraft. She wrote reams of letters copied from her journal where she'd also written loads of polite phrases in French. I only know this because she told me so. She wanted us to go to Europe to practise diplomacy, to bring back secrets. We had to know French for that. My aunt wanted us to watch people and then record it all. She wanted us to make allies and alliances as monarchs did and build future relationships with families called 'Grosjean' and 'Cavin' and 'LaFrance'. She called it 'making contacts'.

Making contacts began in the notebook she kept under her bed, the long list of names and addresses and phrases that began with 'Comment allez-vous?' 'Comm-on-tal-lay-vu': you always had to say that, whether you meant it or not, so you might as well practise saying it in your notebook, or your journal, or your diary, whatever you wanted to call those pages where you wrote things that sometimes embarrassed you. It didn't matter. Nobody would guess your plan. Nobody, my aunt said, could guess 'the machinations of the mind'. Not even your diary. Not even Cardinal Wolsey, and that was his job.

*

Politics is a career full of perks, and politicians cling to perks as they do to power. Political diaries might be regarded as just another unnecessary privilege. What politician, after all, has time to keep a diary; surely they must have something better to do? And yet, in the shifting world of politics, a diary can hold the sorts of secrets and dangerous leakages that might just save political face.

Diarists frequently brag and perhaps political diarists more than any other. Position, after all, is what counts in the political scene, because position means power and power privilege. Who you share or don't share a bathroom with can mean something. Writing from his Parisian apartments in 1782, John Adams sounds like a petty schoolboy: 'Mr. Lauren's Appartments at the hotel de York are better than mine, at the hotel du Roi.'[144] Adams's complaints and comparisons in rank and privilege sound remarkably similar to Pepys's parading of new acquisitions. Pepys loves his coach, often mentioning it more than once in later entries. Travelling by coach indicates a significant rise in social status, marking him out as a man of good fortune. When he purchases his first pair of coach horses he is 'ever maister of', he is sure to tell his diary.[145] On the Twelfth Day of Christmas he travels three times by coach, including to the Duke of York's house and to the theatre.[146] Delighted with his new form of transport, entire days seem to revolve around opportunities for being seen out in his coach. Much time is spent considering what to wear.

By May 1669 he is painting his own fashionable family portraits, carefully constructing the modern equivalent of *Hello!* magazine-style photographs. In his summer suit, Pepys appears as a well-dressed lord complimenting his lady's 'flowered tabby gown'. The effect is kingly and no doubt he wishes there were a crowd. Sure enough, Pepys takes his carriage out, sporting horses with tails tied with red ribbons and laced with green reins. People gather and stare at Pepys-the-personage passing by.[147] Pepys has made it. Such achievement is the result of careful diplomacy and politicking. The two, of course, are related. Without Pepys's cultivated understanding of the political scene none of this would be possible. His career would have foundered, his income cut off.

Pepys's diary tells the story of his career, one embedded in political events and historic moments. As a story it goes pretty well. Already by the spring of 1666, the year of the Great Fire – yet to come – Pepys is boasting to his diary of his considerable rise in status and fortune. What he particularly cherishes are those moments of public display: the trip to St George's Chapel, Windsor, by coach. Such moments of public affirmation translate in Pepys's world into happiness:

> And when I consider the manner of my going hither, with a coach and four horses, the servants and a woman with us ... being made so much of ... and then going to Windsor and being shown all that we were there ... and then going home, and all in fine weather, and no fears nor cares upon me, I do think myself obliged to think myself happy.[148]

Pepys is happy because he has transported himself into a world of privilege. The same year he and his wife have their portraits painted by John Hayls. Sitting in an Indian gown especially hired for the occasion, Pepys adopts the pose of a fashionable and wealthy man holding one of his musical compositions in his raised hand. The posture is firm and bulky, sculptural but with just enough levity and light in the eyes and on his piece of parchment, around his white shirt sleeves and cravat, that Pepys appears well lit. Not yet a Member of Parliament – this was to come in 1673 when he was elected to the seat of Castle Rising, Norfolk – Pepys is now a gentleman of distinction: of private and public accomplishments. He is catching the light well.

Pepys loved the feeling of being a luminary. His diary is a series of self-appointed moments in the limelight. More than 200 years on from Pepys, Alan Clark, long-term minister to Margaret Thatcher, admits to the readers of his Diaries that his are real diaries precisely because he flaunts and bares his ego, because he behaves in ways that publicly would be considered gauche, rude and difficult.[149]

*

Clark spends a lot of time feeling and being important. Everywhere and everyone seem ready made to serve him and his ego. Comfort is essential to his mode of politics, so it would seem. On a trip to Brussels he spends a diary entry describing the level of comfort and prestige afforded by the British Embassy, his surroundings indicative of his status in the world. The 'pleasant ex-Rothschild house' with its heavy mahogany furniture attracts Clark. He begins to imagine himself at home here. With time on his hands he paces his bedroom checking himself out in the mirror. He mourns his former good looks. Only one short glib sentence reminds him of his political mission: to talk to his counterparts and get his 'way', which apparently he has already managed to do. Instead, he quickly returns to assessing the quality of his current life, regarding himself as being on 'holiday'. Soon he will have to pack and head home. The Brussels trip is a reminder of those fading halcyon days. Somehow his political career seems to spin out of that 'long, long youth'.[150] Politics is all that is left to him.

Clark is a man of the world and he reads himself as such. What matters most to him is how he is treated by the world. His published diaries run from 1972 to the summer of 1999 when cancer took over. But he began keeping a diary in 1955 when he was in his early twenties. The young egoist simply becomes an older egoist; perhaps he grows a little more politically savvy, but the 'fool' in Clark, as he calls himself on occasion, never really retreats. The news of Michael Heseltine's resignation, for example, as Margaret Thatcher's Defence Secretary, brings out the fool in him. Whooping with delight at the news, he misreads the situation and then, as is quite common with Clark, second-guesses himself. He shouldn't have told Peter Morrison in the Department of Trade and Industry because at the precise moment when Clark was on the phone to Morrison, Morrison's office was breaking the news to him. Clark's timing is off, and cabinet politics, if nothing else, rests on delicate timings. He ends up feeling 'demi-stupid'.[151]

Clark's *Diaries*, perhaps one of the great documentary accounts of modern political celebrity, is another Game of Life fantasy. Through the ring of telephones and whispers behind closed doors, drama breaks out: news of resignations and cabinet shuffles, the snakes and ladders game of contemporary political life. Yet Clark's diaries reveal a man deeply attached, like Orwell, to rural life. Quite often, he appears a reluctant politician: a man who would rather spend time pursuing his aristocratic hobbies: 'cars, trading, dogs, peacocks',[152] whooshing around in a fast car with a pretty girl, or sitting within his beloved bailey at Saltwood Castle, his family seat. Admittedly, his version of the rural is grander, closer to a stately home than to Orwell's Hertfordshire cottage.

Clark is a man in love with the past; the present seems to ask too much of him. His diaries indulge a habit for nostalgia that allows him enough room for complaining about his present responsibilities. Clark's is a Thatcherite version of Britain and of a private life that encourages the diarist to dream about those days when one had less and went without – 'those early distant happy days' when he and his wife had 'babies' and a blue Oldsmobile.[153] Clark's diaries fuel this fantasy. The present is always less desirable than the past. What one has now – though grander than the past – is a poorer version of what one had then.

*

At the beginning of his political career, May 12th 1972, and the day before his interview for the local parliamentary seat, Alan Clark is to be found sitting in the bay window of the Duke of Cornwall Hotel, Plymouth. Instead of rousing the parliamentarian within, he lapses into a long reminiscence of his last visit to Plymouth, when his wife Jane was rushed to the local hospital. The entry says everything about Clark's relationship to himself, his diary and his political life. Politics is only a means to a public identity; he would rather doodle daydreams and personal reminiscence, remembering the grand house of Nancy Astor, razed during the war.

As he idles in this 'comfortable old fashioned hotel', Clark's diary is his equally idle companion.[154] Public duty calls, but his diary offers a means of shirking the present political moment for a more mellow and modest past. Clark is happy to drift through provincial backwaters. It is hard not to read Clark's diarising as just another gentlemanly pursuit. Political time is urgent. The time of the diary is less so. Diary writing was just another hobby, like his passion for driving and selling fast cars.[155]

*

Diaries privilege the petty. Clark's diary constantly reminds us that it is the petty and the personal that almost always comes first. Diarist and committed socialist Tony Benn confirms this. Benn admits that all diarists, in the end, spin out a 'thin personal story'. Larger events are inevitably filtered and framed through this narrow wedge. A diary can never be regarded as history, however hard the diarist tries to be objective.[156] In 1951, as a New Year's resolution, Benn committed himself to writing what he called a 'political diary'. At least, he tells himself, he will 'try it out'. Distrusting political memoir as a genre, Benn wants his diary to steer away from distortion; he must make sure that memory doesn't warp facts to suit the editorial indulgences of nostalgia.[157]

Telling the News, circa 1982

I lived in a house where people liked to keep track of the news. Some time in the early eighties my aunt started keeping a scrapbook of newspaper cuttings. Every day she sat on her bed in the back room bent over the newspaper, circling the important bits. She took scissors to the circles and cut them out, heads and faces of politicians: Margaret Thatcher waving; Neil Kinnock, a scruffy man in an anorak standing on a windy hill in a place called Beardsley or Barnsley; the Chancellor of the Exchequer – called Nigel – dangling his briefcase from his wrist and smiling through thick lips and bushy brows.

In any case, dates were important, the date at the top of the newspaper, the date when it happened: the miners' strike; the Brighton bomb; Princess Diana smiling and waving in her fairy costume; Mikhail Gorbachev's thinning hair and shiny plastic head. My aunt was saving history, gluing carefully positioned columns of print into tidy rows. She was labelling what was going on in the world, arranging the Important Things, putting current affairs inside a scrapbook she'd bought from WH Smiths in the arcade.

None of us was allowed to touch it. She kept it under her bed with the purple cover pulled down tight. Sometimes when she went to the loo I tugged at that dark place under her bed and felt around; pushed my hands between the layers of crackling dried glue and stiff sugar paper. Beneath the starchy layers I felt the cold, clammy hands of Margaret Thatcher reaching out towards Mikhail Gorbachev as she pretended to smile through her bright red lipstick. Mrs Thatcher always had a handbag. I felt around for the shiny clasps. I knew she'd have a packet of Polos inside like my mum did.

'Always make sure you have a mint on you, Sally. You never know when you might want to sweeten up.' By the time my aunt came back I knew all about Margaret Thatcher's campaign against the miners in Sheffield (or was it Surrey?).

But what was I going to cut out and save? Politics was for adults. That left history, but history was mostly the Tudors and the Stuarts and it came with paintings: lots of portraits of Henry VIII with a big tummy and a belt that barely fitted. I couldn't cut all those out. That would mean cutting up books.

At school we'd made a model of the Falklands Islands from papier mâché, a squishy model made from newspaper that never ever seemed to dry; a paper model cut from news articles that told us all about this 'last bastion of British Rule'. We had to write about it, to keep a news-diary, said Mr Wentworth, 'so we could practise getting the facts right'. But we weren't allowed to use the *Daily Mail* because it told lies.

'Sensationalist right-wing rubbish for people who can't think for themselves.'

My aunt read the *Daily Mail*. She cut it up and saved bits of it inside her scrapbook, reading out loud the important names and dates, the things the politicians said.

'She's very good at summing up things,' said my grand-mother. 'She knows exactly how to cut to the heart of the thing,' said my mother. The heart of the thing sounded bloody and awful, messy, like ripping out the inside of the turkey at Christmas. I didn't want the heart of anything.

'Give a good summary of events,' said Mr Wentworth. 'Check your sources. Don't just rely on one version of events. You'll need to find two or three newspapers, two or three accounts. It's your job to read between the lines and work out what is being said and what might not be. Your news-diary should be impartial. You shouldn't be passing opinion, only observing and reporting on what you hear being reported on.'

'Impartial' sounded like nothing to do with scrapbooking. If you were impartial you couldn't own a pair of scissors; this might encourage you to tell stories in bits, to leave out details, to cut around what you thought was interesting, like how many bridesmaids Princess Diana had had and how many dresses she'd tried on before she found the one she really liked (or the one the Queen liked). No, my scrapbook would have to be made up of parts, only the parts I liked, and instead of commenting on the news I began to make up my own.

*

Political memoirs inevitably serve the political ego. Above all, the politician wants to be remembered well; but he also wants to remember himself well. Labour politician and diarist Chris

Mullin suggests that the best political diaries are written by those who don't make it to the top: he presumably means himself.[158] Benn isn't interested in reminiscence for its own sake. Neither is he keen on massaged memories. He wants accuracy and good recall; he expects his diary to behave like a reliable eyewitness: to record events as they happen and current opinion as it is heard. His diary is to be more a work of cultural history, albeit run through the circumstances of his own life. What it must not be is propaganda, but something closer to tried and tested policy.

The political diarist must lift his subjective head up and take a look at the world around him. Benn's statement of purpose is clear: 'One has to step back a little and assess the changes that are taking place outside.' He soon turns to the events of 'this autumn', November 1957:

> The staggering news in October of the launching of the Russian satellites, Sputnik I and II, has really changed the course of world history. It shows the brilliance of Soviet technology, alters the balance of military power, and more important than either of these two, it marks the beginning of the space age. As long as recorded history exists, 4 October will be remembered and remarked upon. It is far more momentous than the invention of the wheel, the discovery of the sail, the circumnavigation of the globe, or the wonders of the industrial revolution. Looking at the political situation there are not so many momentous events to report.[159]

Benn writes with the sure conviction that this moment in time is full of significance. Sputnik is a historic and global event that will shift the world order. But who will be recording this moment, and how? Journalists cannot be relied upon. As a diarist, Benn feels he must produce robust, coherent political reportage.

In 1951, aged twenty-six, he decides that political life is significant enough to warrant writing it down. As a newly elected Member of Parliament for Bristol South-East, he is suddenly surrounded by political luminaries; the opportunity for bumping into Winston Churchill in the Members' loo is not uncommon.[160] But this, he hastens to remind himself, is just one of the odd perks of the job.

Political Soap Opera

We expect political journals to write of 'events'. Alan Clark captures the lightning bolts of political change striking moment to moment, the urgent business of cabinet reshuffles. Clark writes this up as political soap opera: such as the moment when he finds out he is to become a Tory minister, on June 13th 1983. As with many similar moments, the drama begins and ends with a telephone call. Clark's entry reads as a piece of political Hitchcock:

> It was Ian Gow [Margaret Thatcher's Parliamentary Private Secretary] who telephoned. I had been getting more and more irritable all day as the 'junior' appoint- ments were leaking out on to TV screens, and had taken refuge on the big Atco. I was practically on the last stripe when I saw Jane [Clark's wife] coming across the lawn with a grin on her face. But when she said it was Ian I thought he must be ringing to console me. Surely it's the

Whip who gives the news? And even then a slight sinking feeling at his words, 'The Prime Minister wants you to join the Government.' – 'Go on.' 'It's not what you wanted.' But still a certain delight when he actually enunciated the title, 'Parliamentary Under-Secretary of State at the Department of Employment.'[161]

In a *Dial M for Murder* fashion, the phone comes to signify power, glamour and potential sabotage. Clark makes a call to newly appointed Trade and Industry Secretary Norman Tebbit (admittedly not an obvious source of glamour) who needles him about pulling the ministerial short straw. But glamour soon arrives. Shortly after putting the phone down on Tebbit, his new private secretary Jenny Easterbrook rings to announce herself and the secretarial car. She picks up her new minister and takes him to Brooks's for dinner, gathering a 'coven' of women along the way.

Phone calls keep coming in. The Hon. Peter Morrison and the MP for Northwich ring with polite warnings: Jenny Easterbrook is very pretty; Clark is not to lay a finger on her. Later that evening, driving past the Ritz, one of the 'coven' suggests taking a bed there for the night. The glamour heats up. Clark's 'new life' has begun.[162]

Smart cars, pretty girls, a flashy club: there is a thriller plot here, that continues across the next few days. Clark is fixated on Jenny Easterbrook, and his entry two days after his trip to Brooks's begins with a description of Jenny as a glamorously cinematic blonde: 'Jenny Easterbrook has a very pale skin and large violet eyes. Her blonde hair is gamine short, her sexuality tightly controlled. She makes plain her feelings on several counts (without expressing them).'[163] What follows, rather generously on Clark's part, is Jenny's very low opinion of Clark as both man and cabinet minister.

By June 1995, the telephone is still ringing incessantly. Jane, Clark's 'other woman', his equivalent of Scottie in Hitchcock's *Vertigo*, the woman who stands by him as confidante and ideal wife, rings to tell him that Douglas Hurd has resigned as Foreign Secretary. Moments before (time in Clark's diary seems to tick by in moments), Clark had been in despair about the 'turn of events': Conservative leader John Major's resignation and then immediate offering of himself for re-election. Clark's party is in turmoil and at this moment Clark conceives himself as utterly 'impotent'.[164] His only source of power lies with his diary. Here, at least, he can stoke dreams and fantasies.

'Yesterday was fantasy, euphoria,' Clark writes earlier the same month. The fantasy element refers to a day of indulgent self-imagining. The make-believe begins with a cab ride to Chelsea in which the driver strikes up a conversation about the lack of 'panache' in the Tory leadership. Clark, delightedly, jumps on this: 'Well... who do you fancy?' he asks the bashful cab driver. 'Oh, really? Go on.' The cab driver predictably replies, 'You.' Clark reads the response as a sort of Halley's comet: 'It was a real sign. He was serious and I was serious.'[165] This is either pure political portentousness or a schoolboy's crush; either way, it is effective canvassing.

Clark's diary shores up stories he can savour in private. His political fantasies are closely related to his private fantasies; often the two seem intimately bound. At the same time as he is mourning the demise of his political fortune, he is canvassing hard for the sale of his precious bronze Degas dancer, a significant part of his private fortune. Meanwhile, he reminds himself how often he is recognised out and about in London, how close he hovers to that elusive category of 'celebrity'.

Writing Policy

Tony Benn, on the other hand, has much more of a diary conscience. He has purpose, a mission; he wants to become a better politician, a more effective parliamentarian. Most of his entries are directed away from himself and towards the political process. Benn is writing policy. He observes political shenanigans and takes good note.

After Labour's defeat in the election of 1955, Benn turns to his diary for a post-mortem. What happened? Benn asks. His seat is safe but Labour has clearly got the cultural climate very wrong. Britain is enjoying an economic boom. Rations have ended and a family living in a council house can now afford a TV and a car on hire-purchase.[166] Why on earth would anyone vote anything but Tory? Benn runs a debate with himself, his version of *Question Time*. He summarises his argument thus: one political era has ended and another has begun. Gone is the era of 'petition, indoor meetings, 100 canvasses'. The party will have to find new methods.[167] Despite his claim to the 'thin personal story', Benn sticks with remarkable tenacity to the subject of politics. His diary persona is 'the Party', whose point of view he admirably sustains. Meetings, often heated and irate, and intense negotiations, either with the public or with colleagues, form the substance of his days.

By 1966 Benn is a member of the Labour cabinet (Minister of Technology) and writing with a global view of politics. Television begins to play a large part in his political reality, alongside a constant report on the opinions of the newspapers. Many of his entries begin with media commentary. Nixon's final broadcast as President is the subject on August 9th 1974. Benn describes it as a 'public execution', fascinating to watch.

Despite Benn's protestations to the contrary, he is writing history – from the point of view of a British parliamentarian but also as a regular television viewer. Nixon's farewell speech later that evening makes for 'emotional' viewing.

Politics is a history of the rise and fall of great or lesser men and women. Inevitably, Benn's diary is filled with such ups and downs. Modern political repute is largely formed by the media, and in the blink of an eye, a camera flash, or a brief broadcast, a reputation can be lost and broken. Written on the hoof, in and for the moment, the diary compounds the fleeting quality of political lives. Political history is largely a matter of spectacular moments; at least, what we remember of it. Watching Nixon's farewell address, Benn is struck by the President's likeness to a prime minister who had lost his parliamentary majority. The Watergate scandal is never mentioned. Nixon behaves as though none of that had ever happened. What matters is the pathos of the event. In resigning office, Nixon must win sympathy from his viewers.

We expect good viewing from our politicians and leaders. Pepys seems to think the same. His record of the return of King Charles to English soil is as emotional a reel as Nixon's crushing fall. One man rises, the other falls. Admittedly, Charles's reinstatement is a return from exile. Even at this early point in his career, Pepys is moving close to the powers that be. He proudly records the Duke of York, the King's brother, with whom he conducts 'business' and then seals a future promise of 'favour'. That the duke calls him 'Pepys by name' adds legitimacy to the moment. The sound of 'Pepys' blends into the sound of the crowds whose 'shouting and joy' passes 'all imagination'.[168] We can almost hear the volume turned up, the waving multitudes as the King's coach passes through on the way to Canterbury. Pepys joins the star-struck citizens, waving on the side, his place firmly secured in the moment. Charles's historical reel interrupted ten years ago now begins to replay.

Benn's diary is far less showy than that of Pepys or Clark. In many ways, Benn is writing political policy through observation. His diary is a means of forming and correcting policy through direct experience. He is also writing political history for the sake of posterity. Admittedly, it is his version of history; he decides what is and is not momentous according to his political interests. But Benn is far more interested in the making of policy than Clark or Pepys. He is closer to Adams in his judicious view of how nations and states are built – and upon what. He declares, for example, March 18th 1975 to be a 'momentous' day in the history of Britain. In the cabinet room the matter of the European Economic Community is under discussion. Will the community be a 'supranational structure' or a confederation of sovereign states?

That day, his political colleagues rise to the occasion; the cabinet room is filled with strong speeches and the words of past leaders. James Callaghan gives a persuasive and sensible speech on the need for Europe to remain regional, and quotes Benjamin Franklin.[169] History's great ghosts are used to powerful effect. Benn has a real sense of what constitutes leadership: his diary tracks the scent of political charisma in the formidable form of Mrs Thatcher whom he observes a few months before the crucial cabinet meeting. Here, in the figure of this woman, a momentous history is being born. Benn is quite aware that Thatcher is precisely the sort of woman who could withstand the brutality of politics.

Reading Benn's diaries we are struck by his sense of the truly portentous as opposed to the only imagined. Benn tracks down the big historical questions before they are fully realised.

This is a man paying close attention. A few days on from the Tory leadership election in early February 1975, Benn comments on the mobbing of Mrs Thatcher in Scotland and realises, for the first time, that she appears like the Queen: 'she looks like her, talks like her and is of the same age'.[170] Benn is quite right. A political monarch is emerging.

Benn's talent as a political diarist is his ability to evaluate a day's politics. He understands that certain events carry real weight and grants them such, sloughing off the distractions of negative media attention. Benn is a dedicated negotiator of political policy and his diaries are testament to his sincerity and his political conscience. At the end of the entry, March 18th 1975, he simply writes: 'After that I just needed to unwind.'

John Adams's political maturation takes a similar course. As his political career intensifies, he turns away from the young man who would philosophise about nature. A large bulk of Adams's mid-career diary is devoted to the lengthy negotiations for peace during the American Revolutionary War. Writing from France at the end of 1782 as chief peace-negotiator, commissioned by Congress to sort out Anglo-American disputes, Adams muses out loud on his 'little Negotiations in Europe' as he calls them, and wonders how history might interpret his intense involvement in ending the war.

It is not until he has finally achieved the Peace Treaty of Paris, September 1783, that Adams returns a little more to the man of his youth. Writing from Auteuil, in October 1783, Adams notes the appearance of the woods and landscape from the window of his lodgings. He returns to the picaresque view of the world he held as a young man, to his private imagination, his taste for nature.

Yet this is not a romantic kinship with nature but a politician's pragmatic audit. What Adams does is draw up an inventory of the yield of the land around him. There is no poetry in it; it is rather a list of natural produce and impressive sights: pears, peaches, grapes, châteaux and the Palace of Belle Vue. What is striking about this post-treaty passage is Adams's fixation with land as a form of possession. He notes boundaries, stone walls and gates, the beginning and ending of owned territory on his route through the Bois de Boulogne. Fruit, vegetables and trees are regarded as resources. Gazing out from the window of his chamber, Adams imagines himself lord of a vast estate. His is now a colonial, indeed, an American imagination.[171]

Political Imagining

Political imaginings are almost always bound up with territory, of which constituencies in parliamentary politics are the countable unit. Tony Benn was fighting to continue to hold his constituency in Bristol when his father passed away; with his elder brother dead, Benn suddenly found himself Viscount Stansgate. Thus, Benn was required to sit in the House of Lords. His implementation of the Peerage Act in 1963 returned him to the House of Commons. When the Stansgate business appears in his diaries it is, like the rest of Benn's private life, small and insignificant: a three-day slot in which Benn does nothing but sit in the sun. Stansgate is not political work so 'nuff said'.[172] Land and territory do not feature in Benn's political imagination. He rejects the image of the idle lord, the role of Little Lord Fauntleroy that Clark seems to cherish so much. While Clark basks in the oceans of space afforded to him at Saltwood Castle, Benn reins in the space of his privilege.

*

Diaries naturally betray personal ambition and just as Benn sees Mrs Thatcher as a queen-in-waiting, a force to be politically reckoned with, so Clark, longs to pounce upon the 'queen's' favour at every opportunity. Hovering around the lady he plays Walter Raleigh to Elizabeth, hoping that he can find the right words, the poetry, when she calls.

An extended entry from July 1984 illustrates this perfectly. Clark has been hanging around all morning waiting for the telephone to ring. The weather is 'foully hot' and his head buzzes with mad rumours: 'maddest of all is that Geoffrey Howe will be sacked'. Gazing out from his hot room in the Commons, Clark sees matters only from his own perspective. He is wilfully self-centred, as though to do anything else might cause him damage. Bad temper hangs in the air, waiting to explode. Clark holds a debate with himself, going through all the possibilities should Howe go. Who would be Foreign Secretary? he asks. The answer can only be found in projection and fantasy, a common sport for Clark. Disappointed by the lack of news delivered by his office, Clark can only sit and wait and concoct his schemes.

There is an interval and then the phone rings. The Hitchcock plot is about to resume. Clark knows that it's the 'harsh-voiced' telephone operator from 10 Downing Street. She barks orders at him: hold the line for the Prime Minister. An eternity passes. The operator comes back and tells him that the Prime Minister will call back. Another nervous hour of fantasising passes. Finally the phone goes again:

> 'Alan, I want you to go to Defence.'
> I said nothing.
> Her voice flattened in tone. 'As Minister of State.'
> 'Who is going to be Secretary of State?'
> 'Well, don't tell anyone, because it hasn't been released yet, but Tom [King] is coming back from Ireland to do it.'

Hearing this, Clark's political fantasies plummet. The petulant schoolboy in him blusters back:

> 'I'm sorry Prime Minister, but I can't work with Tom. I went through all of that when I was at DE. I can't do it again. He's too ghastly to work with.'

Clark's resistance to the PM is as puny as a schoolboy's:

> 'I know what you mean, but he is much better now.'
> 'I just can't do it I'm afraid.'
> 'Alan, you've always wanted to go to Defence. I've stood out to get you this job. (uh?) You can't let me down by refusing it.'
> 'Oh all right then, Prime Minister, thank you very much.'
> 'Right then, that's settled.'[173]

The phone goes down.

This is the stuff of *Yes, Prime Minister!* Clark's expertly scripted scene has all the pacing of excellent sitcom writing. It fulfils Benn's 'momentous' criteria although it relates entirely to Clark's career; the state of the nation is very much in service to the state of the man. Politics is there to serve Clark's career rather than the other way around. You couldn't call this a sharp piece of politicking, but it is a good piece of writing and a wonderful insight into the political exertions of the Tory monarch upon her minions. The voice of the Prime Minister is sharply realised, her presence pressing down upon the phone as, vocally, she arm-wrestles Clark into a corner. She's got him the job and he will take it. And like a good boy, he does.

Political History, Political Memory

Reading Benn, Clark, Adams and Pepys, we taste the piquant flavours of their political cultures. In the case of Clark, this is a verbal culture and a verbal reality, scripted to some extent, but largely improvised. It is an aural history vividly captured in diary-reportage, conveying the speed and breathlessness of the political moment in which the fortune of an individual – mainly Clark himself – is determined: in the blink of an eye. Mrs Thatcher sweeps in; Mrs Thatcher sweeps out.

John Adams uses his diary less dramatically but perhaps more seriously: to take notes on political debates, but also to draft aspects of policy. His notes on the Continental Congress of 1776 seem the most portentous, the most crucial, and from these he begins to draft fragments of articles. Verbal statements and persuasive arguments must be recalled but so too must the words of other eloquent men. In February 1776 he remembers the words of Jeremiah: '3. Jer. 12. Go proclaim these Words towards the North. Return thou backsliding Israel and I will not cause my anger to fall upon you, for I am merciful and will not be angry forever.'[174] Before he can find the right words himself he must hear something good; conjure eloquence from other sources, find authority and inspiration. Adams's diary functions as an echo chamber through which he loops rhetorical soundbites: his own voice prompting him to think and so to write. Spurred on by rhetoric, Adams can muster the morale to ask the big constitutional questions: what should America call itself in relation to Great Britain: 'rebells' or 'dutiful subject'?[175] What Adams sounds out in his diary is the stuff of constitutions. There are several takes.

*

Political history, perhaps more than any other form of history, is made up of spoken words, rhetoric, debates turned into written policy made more important on paper. This is the process of policy-making. But there is another form of political history that comes out of politics, what we might call politicking: the live action and drama of individuals running rings around each other.

Despite her own brilliance in the ring, in the end Thatcher is outmanoeuvred by numbers. Too many turn on her; there are too many punches. Clark brilliantly records the live sense of her fall, served up with an expert sense of pace. It is this extended episode that really makes Clark's diary what is perhaps one of the best realisations of political history as it happens. His blow-by-blow account sounds more like radio drama or a Victorian serial thriller, privileging an individual and psychological shift in mood and morale. We are fed the drama in tantalising parts, extended soundbites and dramatic flashes. Naturally, the drama is filtered through Clark and his career concerns; but more than this, his diary provides what sounds like a daily report from a war-zone. Thatcher's fall is a form of guerrilla warfare and it is hard not to compare it with the reports given on Iraq by Clark a few months earlier. 'The Iraqis are starting to throw their weight around,' is beginning to sound familiar.[176]

These days of late 1990 are long days. They begin early and end late. Mostly they begin with a statement on general dissent: 'The Party is virtually out of control. Mutinous. People are not turning up for divisions. Dissidents get bolder and bolder with their little off-the-cuff TV slotettes. Code is abandoned. Discipline is breaking up.'[177] And: 'The whole house is in ferment. Little groups, conclaves everywhere. Only in the dining room does some convention seem to have grown up (I presume because no one trusts their dining companions) that we don't talk shop.'[178] It sounds like a public school slipping into anarchy, or a version of William Golding's *Lord of the Flies*; nowhere is there any sense of good practice.

Clark is describing the fall of a regime and crucially he must decide what side he is on. A respectable period of time should pass before Clark switches allegiance, if it comes to that. Clark is describing a relatively short timescale: the first three weeks of November 1990. On November 4th Clark writes: 'The papers are all very bad. Tory party falling apart, the death blow... something in it, I fear, unless we can get a grip on it.'[179] By November 21st Clark is predicting the 'Longest Day' in politics. Matters have reached a head. Time and space have slowed down. Despite the approaching winter, days have become longer. The diary havers with uncertainty.

Clark needs to find a new game plan now that the 'whole edifice' around the lady is 'in ruins'. He wakes up on the morning of November 21st with his head filled with such thoughts and begins to reckon with history, counting off the years:

It's quite extraordinary. Fifteen years have gone by and yet those very same people...who have always hated her and the values she stood for, are still around in the lobbies, barely looking any different, grinning all over their faces – 'At last we've got her'.

I can't think of a single anti-Thatcherite who has died or receded throughout that entire period.

By 6.30 my tea was cold and I had read the papers.

The papers take Clark back again through the years. Once more, he recalls history and remembers what counts, or at least what did count. A faithful servant to his Queen, he tries to shrug off the present discontents: 'The Party may be just entering on one of its periodic bouts of epilepsy.'[180]

Later that day, Clark drags himself to Whitehall where he finds 'no work being done'. He continues reporting on his very long day; there is a 'general sense of disintegration now affecting everything'. Time drags on and we feel that we are there with Clark: restless, impatient, fretting, desultory. The day is broken up into vignettes. In the third of these, Clark walks over to the House of Commons to be greeted with an announcement from the Prime Minister: 'I fight, and I fight to win.' She is still rallying her troops.

Clark creeps about the corridors of the Commons and listens to the whispering of uncertain dissenters. There is something of the sci-fi genre in these encounters: groups of scrabbling aliens, 'chaps' whose life on earth as they have known it is pretty much at an end.[181] Clark begins to strategise seriously. His diary suddenly becomes less novelistic, less journalistic and more of an urgent problem-solving exercise: pure emergency thinking. Clark shuts off discursive thinking. He needs a plan.

Time and space are broadly dispersed across this 'Longest Day'. At times we feel as if we're locked into a classical drama with a swelling antiphonal chorus. Voices from one side of the stage shout out, 'She could still win' and on the other, 'We've had it'. These are the voices playing loudly inside Clark's head. Shortly after, the scene switches to an Indian restaurant where Clark has taken time out to write up 'the traumatic happenings' of the evening. We realise that something has happened in between and he is now looking back to the more recent past, earlier that evening: his pathetic encounter with the Prime Minister in which he tries, once again, to win her over. And again, he fails:

> She looked calm, almost beautiful. 'Ah, Alan ...'
>
> 'You're in a jam.'
>
> 'I know that.'
>
> 'They're all telling you not to stand, aren't they?'
>
> 'I'm going to stand. I have issued a statement.'
>
> 'That's wonderful. That's heroic. But the party will let you down.'
>
> 'I am a fighter.'
>
> 'Fight then, fight to the end, a third ballot if you need to. But you lose.'
>
> There was quite a little pause.
>
> 'It'd be so terrible if Michael [Heseltine] won. He would undo everything I have fought for ...'
>
> Outside, people were doing that maddening trick of opening and shutting the door, at shorter and shorter intervals.
>
> 'Alan, it's been so good of you to come in and see me.'[182]

Clark withdraws with a familiar sense of failure. All he wants is for things not to change; like a small child who longs for the continuing presence of his mother but who knows, inevitably, she will go away and leave him.

The day ends with a thrilling sight: at half past eight Clark passes through the exit to Speaker's Court where he meets with the Prime Minister's Jaguar. The car door slams, the interior light goes off and the car 'slid away'. Clark is left standing alone in the dark considering his destiny. History hurtles before him but also the nature of political life that has swaddled him for so long: such is the myopia of 'so many in public life'.[183]

Clark feels like an orphan without his mother. Political history has thwarted his good intentions. This is more than a personal diary: it is a truly historic moment as well as a moment of sincere contemplation. We feel as if something genuine has passed between the diarist and us, his curious reader. In this moment we feel, fleetingly, a small ache of sympathy for his circumstances. This is either brilliant politics or very good writing. Either way, we are convinced of its validity because Clark has confessed to something unkindly true.

CHAPTER SIX:

WAR AND DISASTER

The person we meet in Clark's diaries is convincing precisely because he narrates emergencies almost entirely through the prism of his own character. This is what we expect of his diaries, perhaps of all diaries: the person before politics, the politics of the person.

Clark can be careless and casual about political events. Politics appear and disappear according to his whim. Politics re-emerges only when things begin to get critical. In March 1982 the Falklands War suddenly appears in his journal. Clark gives us no real critical cause, only a coarse description of the war's beginning that sounds remarkably similar to Ronald Reagan's cowboy-cum-sheriff routine:

> A bunch of Argentinians are horsing around in Georgia. The thing started as an operation to retrieve 'scrap' (by what right do they go in there and remove 'scrap' anyway?). But they have now apparently hoisted the Argentinian flag. I don't like this. If we don't throw them out, preferably shedding blood at the same time, they will try their hand in the Falklands.[184]

When news of an Argentinian invasion finally breaks, Clark responds like a sulking schoolboy (again); he is the last to know. Returning to Saltwood that evening, he reports to his wife on the state of affairs, with more than a schoolboy's touch of drama: '"We've lost the Falklands," I told Jane. "It's all over. We're a Third World country, no good for anything."' Jane suitably doesn't respond.

*

'Humankind cannot bear very much reality,' T. S. Eliot reminds us. In the face of war or despotism as he sees it, Alan Clark shuffles off for an evening walk.[185] Wars, of course, are largely battles for the best intelligence, and diaries can serve as valuable containers for turning such information over. The best intelligence can lead to the shrewdest decisions. Today's bloggers compete for attention from a mass of online readers, all hankering after information. A blogger, like a good soldier, must have good, reliable information. The blog and the diary offer a practical space for strategizing. Sometimes they can encourage us, crucially, to falter and hesitate. A diary can be witness to overwhelming moral decisions.

Faced with the awful prospect of atomic warfare, US President Harry Truman turned to his diary in an attempt to map out a sensible mental route: to bomb or not to bomb the Japanese? A diary entry from early December 1945 records his firm decision. Truman will bomb, but he will bomb selectively. He delivers the decision to himself like a fatal omen:

We have discovered the most terrible bomb in the history of the world. It may be the fire destruction prophesied in the Euphrates Valley Era, after Noah and his fabulous Ark ... The weapon is to be used against Japan between now and August 10th. I have told the Sec. of War, Mr. Stimson, to use it so that military objectives and soldiers and sailors are the target and not women and children. Even if the Japs are savages, ruthless, merciless and fanatic, we as the leader of the world for the common welfare cannot drop this terrible bomb on the old capital or the new... It seems to be the most terrible thing ever discovered, but it can be made the most useful.[186]

Truman's casual entry is frightening to read. Convincingly judicious of tone, the President seems to have talked himself into the rightfulness of bombing. Such a weapon might be 'useful', and despite the triple repeat of the bomb's 'terrible[ness]', the Japanese are four-fold terrible: savage, ruthless, merciless and fanatic. The bomb is the only solution.

Truman's calm is unnerving; but his decision has been made and his diary stands as his witness to the process. Six months earlier he writes: 'I have to decide Japanese strategy – shall we invade Japan proper or shall we bomb and blockade? That is my hardest decision to date. But I'll make it when I have all the facts.'[187] His diary will gather up all the facts and talk through them. In the tradition of state counsellor, his diary holds the post of senior adviser.

*

Writing at the outbreak of the Second World War, Virginia Woolf waits, along with the rest of Britain, for news of Hitler's escalating threats and tantrums. She wants news, but she wants it to be sure and certain, free of gossip. She addresses her diary as a silent companion, a reliable witness, someone she can speak out loud to, someone to whom she can pose

unanswerable questions: 'Ask what will be happening this time
10 days? Suppose we skim across, still at any moment, any
accident may suddenly bring out the uproar.' And although it
remains silent, her diary seems to carry a voice, a character, a
speaking, reassuring presence.

Woolf continues to speak to her diary as she speaks to herself: 'And as we're all equally in the dark we can't cluster &
gossip; we are beginning to feel the herd impulse; everyone
asks everyone, Any news?'[188] Here, in her diary voice, we hear
the sound of someone thinking aloud, part public announcement, part private musings; a style that merges inner and outer worlds. When we read any of her diary entries we hear a
direct address, as though Woolf were reading her thoughts out
loud to herself at the same time as she writes them down.
Woolf would like to be speaking and writing at once, for words
to fall upon the page as she utters them. Hers is an interior
monologue with good acoustics; we can hear what she says
and she seems to be including us.

Meanwhile, she clings to an account of reality that unfolds
moment to moment. Her countdown to war reads: 'Wednesday
30 August: Not at war yet. Par[liamen]t met yesterday.
Negotiations. We are firm ...' Then on Friday, September 1st
she writes: 'War is on us this morning. Hitler has taken
Danzig: has attacked or is attacking – Poland.' And then,
finally, on Sunday, September 3rd: 'This I suppose certainly
the last hour of peace.'[189]

While Orwell divides the political situation into three
distinct social realms, Woolf sees nothing as separate from her
own life. She writes her private telegram on the shifting state
of the nation from her living room, as it comes to her through
the radio. These passages are filled with nerves that jitter and
jump all over the place, nerves to-ing and fro-ing from 'no

war' to 'war', and finally to a sentence that fades upon an ellipsis: 'Otherwise quiet & usual eno.' By now Woolf is talking to herself. Her broken sentences are the mutterings and murmurings of half-uttered thoughts, of a mind anxiously circling. The sound of the radio draws her back into the world of war news, but she can only make mental fragments from it. Nothing coherent. By September 3rd 1939 Woolf's diary is mainly what language theorist Stephen Pinker might call mentalese: the stuff of private thought.[190]

*

'War news more or less meaningless,' English novelist and socialite Evelyn Waugh tells his diary six months on from Woolf's entry.[191] A few days prior to this, Waugh brazenly declares his intention to remain 'the only English family to eschew the radio throughout the crisis'. He quickly returns to the business of home and garden: the 30-foot Gothic balustrade and the weed-heap.[192] In a time of crisis, we can really only deal with what we know: the close and the familiar, the habitat of the heart.

Yet, despite his protestations to the contrary, Waugh does eavesdrop on the wireless: in Mrs Lister's motor car outside the village hut (in Stinchcombe, Gloucestershire), while waiting for child evacuees. Although the wireless assures its listeners that the evacuation plan is running like 'clockwork', no children arrive. Waugh reminds us that part of the diarist's pleasure is regular access to a space in which he can pass uncontested opinions. Diaries are silent listeners, nodding affirmation and assent; and so Waugh smugly reiterates his original opinion: that news heard on the radio is unreliable. Ignore it and carry on.[193]

War inevitably brings muddles, and in such circumstances a diary can serve as a useful filter for the stream of public information. Evelyn Waugh spends a great deal of time waiting for news – in his particular case, news of a military appointment that would drag him from sleepy Stinchcombe. For George Orwell, a diary was a useful tool for sorting through public sources. But like any good journalist, and one particularly sensitive to the effect of propaganda, Orwell handles all information circumspectly:

> 29.5.40: One has to gather any major news nowadays by means of hints and allusions. The chief sensation last night was that the 9 o'clock news was preceeded by a cheer-up talk... by Duff-Cooper [Minister of Information] to sugar the pill. Churchill said in his speech ... that the house must prepare for 'dark and heavy tidings'.[194]

As an astute political journalist, Orwell uses his wartime diary to try to make political sense of the world and to determine what the future of Europe, as it is crudely divined and defined by the media, might look like. In the meantime, there is an awful lot of paper to wade through. His days are spent checking information: what it is that the *Star*, the *Evening News* and the *Evening Standard*, the *Daily Worker and Action*, the *Tribune* and, in particular, the *Daily Telegraph* are printing. His diary is an overwhelming political project, and contrasts sharply with the record of those same days made by his contemporary, Waugh, mainly in the distinction between Orwell's breathlessly contingent domestic life and the emerging international political situation.

On the last day of August 1939 he not only provides a full

bulletin-report on the political status quo from three points of view – 'Foreign and General', 'Social' and 'Party Politics' – but also gives us a broadcaster's soundbite on the blackberries of Hampshire. It is an absurd juxtaposition of events, but one that is true to life; that is to say, true to Orwell's view of life as a political journalist: one tidily compartmentalised.

*

While Orwell discusses disaster at a distance, Pepys has to face it head-on. On the morning of September 2nd 1666 London woke to the devastating effects of a Great Fire. Pepys, in fact, woke earlier than most, at 3 am. Faced with the horrifying sight of pigeons and even stonework 'proving combustible', he determines to act quickly. News must be got out, and, like an action-adventure hero, he jumps into a boat and paddles along the Thames to Whitehall where he presents himself at the King's chamber with the news that London is on fire.[195]

For Pepys, the fire meant a call to action; as it turned out, it was an event in which he played chief newsmonger and messenger. Pepys is in his element; disaster sweeps through London and he is at the centre of the action. More than this, he is put in charge, instructed by the King and the Duke of York to inform the Lord Mayor to pull down houses. Suddenly, Pepys is London's grand disseminator of information, in charge of the mayor and all public decisions – running a campaign to save his city, or so it would seem. His account of the fire is lavishly medieval and dramatic, the written equivalent of fifteenth-century artist Hieronymus Bosch's triptych, The Last Judgment. It is a pictorially rich and detailed account of the multitude of scrambling bodies tumbling through the

London streets with their 'good goods' in carts and barrows. Bodies pour down streets like hordes of desperate rats fleeing the persecution of pursuing flames.

Pepys himself is forced into rather desperate actions: he takes his valued goods into the back garden, and his gold and 'chief papers' to his office, ready to carry away. The scene could have been lifted from a seventeenth-century city comedy – Ben Jonson's *Volpone*, for instance – except that Pepys, the devoted administrator, is more conscientious than Jonson's scoundrel: as concerned with saving his account papers as he is his gold.[196]

On the scale of disaster, the Great Fire is the largest Pepys describes. Personal history is suddenly buried away for the sake of this large-scale piece of reportage. Yet small human pleasures and desires are always mentionable in Pepys's world, his diary existing, in part, to highlight the small, snug moment as much as the panoramic view of history. In the middle of the fire he reports on a personal 'design' of his to show off the contents of his 'closet' to his friend, Mr Moone. This 'long-desired' event is thwarted by the more pressing circumstances of the fire; Pepys is disappointed. He had wanted to show off his private space, the seventeenth-century equivalent of a male den and the place he keeps his treasures – his homemade bookshelves and the commissioned portrait of himself.[197]

Daily life is made up of small details, many vain and unnecessarily decorative. Pepys's closet might serve as a metaphor for the diary: a storage space for personally selected signs and symbols that, over several days, and with some rummaging and sorting, might be arranged into coherent stories.

My Grandmother's Little Red Notebook

I never really learned what my grandmother kept in her little red notebook, the one she got from Woolworth's in the precinct or the stationer's next to the greengrocer's. She used it mostly for her shopping lists, single words stacked in a wonky pile going up and down the page.

Milk – 12 pints
Bread – 3 farmhouse
Butter – 6pkts
1 Bnch Bananas
Ravioli – 6 tins
Tea – 2 pkts
Marmalade
Weetabix
Bacon – 3 pkts
Sausages – 3 pkts

Sometimes we stole her notebook and added things to her list. Under 'Biscuits' we put: 'NOT Lincoln or gingernuts. Chocolate chip or shortcake please. Or best of all Jam Sandwich creams. DEFINITELY NOT BOURBONS.'

It was hard to read my grandmother's handwriting, which looked as though it might fall off the page. She wrote like an old person. Mum said it was a 'frail hand' which we thought meant her hands might fall off if the list got too long.

Her version of shorthand couldn't have saved much time, as she sometimes left out only one letter. I think that was how she'd been taught to make notes back when she was a secretary. She never wrote complete sentences. At least I don't think she did. I only ever looked at the front, at the list. I didn't peek at the back. Now I wish I had.

I imagined that she kept tennis results there when Wimbledon was on the telly. She loved tennis. She taught us how to serve with my brother's old wooden racket and our soggy green ball. Tennis was part of her secret life, her past, my young grandmother, the grandmother I'd never known but wish I had; the grandmother who had been written over by her notebook, by her list, by my aunt's version of things.

Our days would have been completely different without that small lined red book with big staples down the centre. For one thing, we wouldn't have had tea. And tea happened every five minutes in our house. Tea was what we did when nothing else was going on, which was most of the time.

Now that I think of it, my grandmother's shopping list was probably the most political bit of writing in our house. Food was what made everything happen. Food was the beginning and end of every day: my grandmother sat at our sticky kitchen table with her pencil and notebook twice a day, making a list of groceries for the following day. She called her list her 'ration book' because she remembered the war when there were no bananas. These only became available after the war and were always on her list, 'because you could live on bananas', she said. 'If you were stuck on an island with nothing else, like Robinson Crusoe, you could survive by living off bananas. If there were any... if Man Friday had bothered to order them in.'

We made fun of my grandmother's list, but it was vital, as much, if not more so, than my mum's diary, because she wrote it every day. That list meant we had breakfast, lunch and tea. That list was what made my older brother, over the years, turn six foot four. It was what made me five foot seven and three-quarters.

*

As the sounds of war get louder and closer, Woolf clings to aesthetic reasons for staying alive. The light over her Downland home is still 'evanescent' and 'shining'; the weather is still a subject of rapidly changing beauty. All these are deflections of 'light' from the dark business of war – which, as W. H. Auden suggested in his portentous poem 'September 1st, 1939', work like 'ironic points' on an otherwise flat horizon. Faced with the magnitude of war, the average person clings more stubbornly to their average day.

Woolf clings to beauty because it has always been part of her average day: the nature of the light, the weather, the state of the skies, the state of her mind, the condition of her writing. By early September 1939, war has crept into the 'furniture of home', but it never threatens to raze the 'fort' of everyday life. Although 'the odour of death', as Auden puts it, hangs in the air, Woolf, as most of us would, continues to be obsessed with her private life.[198] The Downs are still beautiful; she still has a chapter to finish.

Woolf's diary is now much closer to a novel or a play, closer to the substance of her final novel, *Between the Acts*. Now there are private and public protagonists as there is private and public tragedy. She is aware of only the thinnest of tissues remaining between both worlds. Writing from her sister's house, Charleston Farmhouse, in Sussex, she senses that invasion is urgent and near. 'The public world notably invaded the private at MH [Monk's House], last week,' she nervously reports. 'Almost war, almost expected to hear it announced.' Public and private spheres see-saw back and forth. 'Suicides' and 'refugees' are being turned back from Newhaven. But in the midst of all the outer turmoil, she senses a 'lull', and in that lull Woolf returns to private losses, to thoughts of her dead nephew, Julian Bell, killed in July of that year. Julian's death seems 'somehow not pointless'. 'I keep thinking why is he not here to see the daffodils; the old beggar woman – the swans,' she muses. These are the private thoughts, prompted by Charleston and its idyllic, pastoral garden.[199]

The word 'lull' reappears in the same entry. 'Lull' is normal, social life resuming in the face of war. It is the superficial business of buying dresses and inviting other novelists to tea. 'Lull' is parties and chitter-chatter. 'Lull' is also a break from full submergence in the writing of her biography, the life of her dead friend Roger Fry, which will return her to the past.[200] Roger is an escape from the horrifying present; he is private history, a tender elegy for times, people and places that have vanished.

Writing Stories Instead of News

My school news-diary was filled with facts and figures, long numbers about troops being sent 'overseas', numbers I copied from the front page of the *Daily Mail*, numbers I pretended to have found somewhere else.

'Overseas' was the word newspapers used when they discussed war and politics. 'Overseas' was filled with 'aircraft' and 'frigates' and 'jets' – 'Harriers' (or was that another war?) and 'Typhoons'. I cut out a diagram that compared how many jets the Argentinians had compared to us. We had more. And in all the pictures printed the Union Jack was the first thing I saw. I think that was the point. I cut one of those out too and stuck it on the front.

The Falklands Islands looked dreary. The newspaper pictures showed nothing there, just bleak hills tipped with snow and straight deserted roads. In the middle of the roads trudged soldiers – 'our soldiers' we called them – in faded green-grey uniforms. No animals, no trees, no sun, nothing, I thought. What's the point in fighting over this place? What's even there?

Mr Wentworth said something about 'oil reserves', but by then I had stopped listening. I was doodling, turning my Berol pen around and around on the same page, filling it up with ink. I wanted to write. The Falklands War had nothing to do with me and it seemed to have nothing to do with most people. It wasn't anywhere anyone would ever want to go on holiday. You wouldn't send your gran a postcard from the Falklands, so why bother? Our papier mâché model standing in the corner of the room looked lumpish and silly, a strange deformed creature from outer space; a lost and lonely Martian.

So I started writing stories in my news-diary about witches and goblins and elves and little folk who lived under stairs. I wanted to be like Mary Norton and Beatrix Potter and Enid Blyton, a woman with a bold name printed on the front of a book in letters that made people stop and look; I wanted to write a book that people would pick up and smell, as I'd smelled the pages of my books when I first opened them: to the first sentence, the first word, the first arresting name, the first character I could grab hold of and 'do a bunk with' as my brother would say.

Years later when I read the words of Cassandra Mortmain I knew that I had been suffering what she suffers from, 'a stillness inside a restlessness', which is perhaps what all writers suffer from: a desire to write yourself out of here and now and go somewhere else, somewhere other than my classroom in Connaught Junior School, Littlehampton-on-Sea, West Sussex, England.

There is no 'on-sea' about it, said my friend Mandy when I

showed her what I'd been writing. 'You're just trying to sound important. And why do you need to say where you are? No one cares. No one cares about your silly stories in your silly diary. Who cares about Connaught Junior School … no one's ever heard of it … or of you … no one's ever heard of any of us and no one ever will … so why do you even bother to write it down?'

Because it mattered that I knew how to be somewhere else and someone else instead of me. But there was no point telling Mandy Gibson that.

'I could hear the rain still pouring from the gutters and a thin branch scraping against one of the windows; but the church seemed completely cut off from the restless day outside – just as I felt cut off from the church. I thought: I am a restlessness inside a stillness inside a restlessness.' (Cassandra Mortmain, some time in the past and the present and the future.)

*

During war, private lives continue: life at home, the life of houses and what to do with them. Evelyn Waugh's opening gambit, during the lead-up to war, is to try to rent out his home. Having purchased Piers Court, Gloucestershire, in 1937, the house and all its 'expensive machinery' quickly turned into an costly encumbrance with the threat of war.[201] He turns to his garden as a way of distracting himself from this fact.

Waugh shares Orwell's passion for garden notes, but unlike Orwell's rather modest cottage garden, Waugh's home at Piers Court is a rather grander affair: tennis courts, driveways and woodland. Still, the sentiment is the same: this is an attempt at an English pastoral. Waugh, above all, is an enthusiast, and

sprinkled through his summer 1939 diary entries are dilettan-
tish notes on home-improvement written in a telegraphic
shorthand: 'Continuous rain. Dug path in woodland'; 'More
rain and tennis court'; 'Church and Spade'. War comes almost
as a break from household duties, and, in typical fashion,
Waugh broaches the experience as another opportunity for
amateur enthusiasm – opening up Piers Court to evacuees
with great gusto.

But this is not enough; what he wants above all is real
employment: a posting in the Ministry of Information or with
one of the armed forces. Bored and restless, he writes on
September 17th 1939: 'Had I no garden to dig in I should be
in despair with lack of occupation.'[202] For Waugh, war is a
'project', and one that challenges his sense of self. As his diary
more than hints at, the threat of invasion incites an identity
crisis as he finds himself repeatedly asking what is it that, as a
novelist and a journalist, he can offer except his large home?
His role as estates manager is not enough, and reading his
diary we meet a man driven to convert his privilege but also
his profession into something more useful.

In the end, Waugh secures a commission in the Royal
Marines through his considerable social connections and gains
the 'war project' he desires.[203] Still, reading Waugh's wartime
diary, we are struck by a strange continuity between pre- and
post-war Waugh. The same things still matter: champagne,
a good luncheon, an effervescent social event. War seems to
offer him all these. Sent to Chatham for preliminary training,
Waugh roamed between one training quarters and another
until finally he was dispatched on the SS Ettrick to West
Africa as part of a campaign alongside General de Gaulle
to take the port of Dakar. The expedition was a spectacular
failure.

Diary Diversions

Nonetheless, Waugh persisted with his war 'projects', transferring to Combined Operations under Colonel Robert Laycock. In February 1941, as Laycock's Intelligence Officer, he sailed to the Libyan coast where he took part in a night raid on German-held Bardia. Between 1942 and 1943, Waugh is permanently stationed in the United Kingdom, and at a loose end. His diary entries read like a novelist in search of a diverting plot and setting, some engaging characters and dialogue. His entry for September 24th 1942 describes a visit to a commando at Dundee. His attention falls mainly upon aesthetics, the grandeur of the commando's pile: 'a great palace with massive Italian terraces, too much shiny white paint, some splendid pictures, mostly Spanish, and a chapel by Boris Anrep'. Next up is their host's wife, an 'extremely pretty and self-conscious' woman.

In the middle of war, Waugh is still assessing the aesthetic value of the place in which he finds himself. He consistently he assess the quality of hospitality on offer, which includes the level of good looks provided by his host and careful observation of social manners and behaviours. This could be a scene from his coming-of-age novel of social manners, *Brideshead Revisited*. We could be in Lady Marchmain's sitting room:

> When Bob and I arrived we were shown into her where she sat over a dead fire in a semi-circular sitting-room. She leapt like a deer, said, 'Oh. I don't know where Bill is. He's always disappearing when strangers arrive,' and fled from the room. Later she played poker dice, wholly absorbed in Bill, and won consistently. Mrs Stirling full of charm and humour.

When death raises its ugly head it causes only embarrassment. There is 'no news of David', whoever David is, and his name is quickly passed over. Waugh's entry is full of the cruel superficiality of social chit-chat, its glib refusal to prioritise a dead man over a round of after-dinner drinks:

> They have heard no news of David; we had heard, but from the doubtful source of Randolph, that he was missing after the Benghazi raid. We held our peace … Basil Bennett brought large quantities of liquor for us. I think we are the only mess in Europe which constantly drinks clarets, port and brandy at dinner.[204]

We are reminded of Woolf's description of dead boys in the First World War suddenly cutting through the mind of Mrs Dalloway as she flits across the room of her party:

> For it was the middle of June. The War was over, except for some one like Mrs. Foxcroft at the Embassy last night eating her heart out because that nice boy was killed and now the old Manor House must go to a cousin; or Lady Bexborough who opened a bazaar, they said, with the telegram in her hand, John, her favourite, killed; but it was over; thank heaven – over. It was June.[205]

Death is another stranger, a rude intruder: 'in the middle of my party, here's death,' thinks Mrs Dalloway.[206] Despite the war, society with all its social configurations continues: parties and love affairs, bazaars and pageants, all the local and exotic arrangements of English social life.

*

Waugh's primary interests are social: good literature, food and liquor, splendid décor and good company. This is his war. In between, he reads and reviews books, but he also writes, and so the war enters his novel world.

Basil Seal, the protagonist of his 1942 novel, *Put Out More Flags*, is chronically bored, his mood precarious, and Waugh shares similar temperamental vacillations. Waugh's diary records his daily vacillations as he lurches between a state of reflective contentment for his thirty-ninth year which has brought him some 'good soldiering among friends', and a deep depression over his lack of a challenging post. His 'peculiar' illness, as he calls it, manifests in 'dreams of unendurable boredom' in which he is forced to read page after page of dull literature. Art, in other words, has become as disappointing as life.[207]

Boredom doesn't kill but it certainly degrades. On the long sail to Dakar, Waugh reports days of hard drinking and playing 'tombola'. Time and space blur beneath a fog of drunken inactivity. A diary becomes a way of holding on to a sense of purpose, of continuous time and space; and here there is some sort of modest courage, for keeping a diary as an active officer was a severe military offence.[208] But Waugh is anxious to be taken seriously as an intelligence officer, and, like Orwell, prides himself on his ability to gather reliable information.

In September 1940 he begins a battalion War Diary as another act of defiance – his intelligence summary having been dismissed as 'superfluous' by his division.[209] There is a fussy and rather petulant side to Waugh's account-keeping, a persona who contradicts the man 'drunk before luncheon'.[210] His 'Memorandum' of July 1940–41 records his experience with the Commandos and includes the Battle of Crete. Waugh is critical of his fellow soldiers and of the campaign in general.

Extra-curricular, extra-official, the memorandum is a clear attempt to take himself seriously as an officer, to write himself into a more soldierly reality. His 'Memorandum' serves as a way of processing what he considers to be the shoddy performance of the officers in charge. He complains about the 'deteriorating' discipline among the men; the 'indolence and ignorance of the officers', which, nonetheless, places them 'slightly above normal army standards'.[211] In the end, Waugh's battalion diary produces a soldier-avatar version of himself, a corrected and improved version of the one living and fighting in real time.

*

Disasters can and do produce celebrities. The Fire of London turns Pepys into an overnight star, taking direct orders from the King himself. Pepys is happy to write himself into the drama as its protagonist; at the same time he assigns himself the function and methods of the dramaturge.

As with all real personalities, Pepys gives us a lot of himself that is not heroic, reminding us that diaries do not ask the diarist to discriminate between the large and small event. Daily affairs wobble along and the grand narrative falls by the wayside.

We all rely upon detail to distract us from emergencies. Reading Pepys we are reminded of ourselves, of human nature in general, our reliance upon petty distractions. You attend to the emergency for as long as is needed and return to the personal story as soon as you can. Pepys's attention shifts back and forth between the petty, the pretty and the pathetic. Positioning himself up high, on the Tower of London, he commands a bird's-eye view of the city. Among other sorry sights he notices dislodged pigeons, 'loath to leave their hous-es, but hovered about the windows and balconies till they were some of them burned, their wings, and fell down'.[212] Pepys's pigeons are an extension of London's citizens, clinging to their homes; those 'poor people' he observes from the Tower top, 'staying in their houses as long as till the very fire touched them'.[213] It is the tenderness of the detail, the smallness of things observed that catches us as we read Pepys's view of London on fire. But Pepys's London is always local and particular. We smile when we hear Pepys delivering a bird's-eye view of London on fire, but without failing to notice what one of his acquaintances is wearing. His eye roams from the large site – London's warehouses – to the smaller losses of Mr Isaccke Houblon, 'that handsome man – prettily dressed and dirty at his door at Dowgate, receiving some of his brothers things whose houses were on fire.'[214] Pepys is a good neighbour: he notices what matters within the small scene, the plight of the little people. We never forget that London is made up of individual citizens: from the King standing amazed in his bedchamber surrounded by concerned staff, to Mr Houblon looking soiled and sorry on the steps of his home.

CHAPTER SEVEN

SCANDAL

Pepys's diary reminds us that there is never a bad time to think of yourself. Nothing is too small or delicate for Pepys, nothing too personal. At the height of one of the worst years in London's history, the year of the Great Plague (1665), when the city is overrun with dead bodies, Pepys is fussing over his wardrobe and wig:

> Lords day. Up, and put on my coloured silk suit, very fine, and my new periwigg, bought a good while since, but darst not wear it because the plague was in Westminster when I bought it. And it is a wonder what will be the fashion after the plague is done as to periwigs, for nobody will dare to buy any haire for fear of the infection – that it had been cut off the heads of people dead before the plague.[215]

It is not London's future but the future of wiggery that is foremost in his mind. Pepys can be a vain man. He is also a man much disposed to making money and being merry. That year, 1665, is a good one for Pepys, as is the following year – both disastrous for London. During these years, Pepys's personal life positively burgeons. Early in 1666 he is found enjoying a Sunday lie-in, an activity interrupted only by the arrival of his new tailor, Mr Penny, bringing him a new 'Camelott cloak'. Pepys makes merry with his journal, vowing to catch up on late entries before he kisses any more women or drinks any more wine. His mood is so buoyant that his flirtation even turns upon his diary.[216] Anyone and everything is a potential source of love-making. An early spring fever sets in along with a promise to 'make merry'. Pepys is bubbling over with the pleasure of increased and increasing prosperity. He continues to work hard on the naval accounts for Tangier, England's colonial port in Morocco – a project that secures his professional reputation – but daily life is now a rich mixture of visits from neighbours, sing-alongs, luncheons and suppers: days and nights of carousing.

In the Wrong Hands

During these years, a racier Pepys is emerging. Indiscreet behaviours begin to creep into his home life. In 1665, in the middle of an after-dinner round of cards, he steals away to his closet with Peg Hughes, an actress in the King's Company, where, he tells his diary, she 'did suffer [me] a la besar mucho et tocar ses cosas upon her breast': in other words, a nice bit of post-prandial kissing and fondling. All this brings much 'pleasure', 'entertainment' and a 'mind mightily pleased'.[217] But Pepys is flirting with scandal. What if his diary got into the wrong hands – a rival at court, or, worse, his wife, who from time to time is one of his closest 'enemies'?[218] Keeping a diary can be a risky business.

Diaries can be treacherous if they get into the wrong hands, and in our contemporary culture of heightened litigation, diaries are the most likely betrayers of their keepers. Evelyn Waugh destroyed several of his Oxford diaries because he considered the material therein potentially scandalous: reflections on his homosexual affairs. 'My diary for the period is destroyed,' he writes to his old school friend, Dudley Carew, confessing that he has been 'incredibly morally depraved'.[219]

In the contemporary world of international politics, diaries are almost banned items. Bill Clinton must have known this. He left no diary traces, only some tapes, as (unfortunately for him) did President Nixon. However, Nixon's Chief of Staff and faithful aide, Bob Haldeman, did leave written traces. In his diaries, published posthumously in 1994, Haldeman meticulously recorded daily life within the White House. Inevitably, his entries let some of Nixon's wayward – or scandalous – views (or 'P' as he calls him in diary shorthand) out of the bag. Take this summary of a discussion of the welfare system:

Got into a deep discussion of welfare, trying to think out the Family Security decision, with E and me (welfare reform had been one of P's campaign issues). P emphasized that you have to face the fact that the whole problem is really the blacks. The key is to devise a system that recognizes this while not appearing to. Problem with overall welfare plan is that it forces poor whites into same position as blacks. Feels we have to get rid of the veil of hypocrisy and guilt and face reality.

Pointed out that there has never in history been an adequate black nation, and they are the only race of which this is true. Says Africa is hopeless, the worst there is Liberia, which we built.[220]

Obviously, these sorts of observations are politically damaging. One wonders why Haldeman chose to record them. His comment shows political naïvety and lack of foresight – or perhaps a commitment to the diary's rule of thumb: that in the giving of information, diaries deliver without discrimination.

But Haldeman is a twentieth century diarist. He should have known better. In the seventeenth century a man could still hope to keep his conscience safe within the bounds of his journal. Pepys's diary is politically naïve. While he may 'discourse' philosophically with his neighbour, Mr Hill, on 'most things of a man's life', each man recognising how 'little merit doth prevail in the world only favour', Pepys nonetheless takes great risks with his domestic life.[221] What he says he does in his diary puts his reputation at risk, and, above all, his marriage. Scandal, of course, can only arise from reputation. But did this ever really worry Pepys? As it was for Clinton, Pepys's libido puts him at risk of the twin demons of blackmail and scandal. But perhaps worst of all is having to face the wrath of Mrs Pepys.

Guilty Secrets and Gossip

Pepys's diary bubbles with guilty secrets; it is hard to imagine how he got away with so many extramarital affairs. But sex, for Pepys, is fun, a form of sport, and when he sees an attractive woman pass him in the street, he convinces himself that she takes a second glance:

Going to Whitehall I had pleasant racontre of a lady in mourning, that by the little light I had seemed handsome;

I passing by her, I did observe she looked back again and again upon me, I suffering her to go before, and it now being duske. I observed she went into the little passage towards the privy water-gate, and I followed, but missed her; but coming back again, I observed she returned and went to go out of the Court. I fallowed her ... to take her by the hand to lead her through, which she willing accepted, and I led her to the great gate and there left her ... but my boy was at the gate, and so yo durst not go out con her – which vexed me; and my mind (God forgive me) did run après her todo the night, though I have reason to thank God, and so I do now, that I was not tempted to go further.[222]

This is the stuff of modern advertisements. It is a piece of narcissistic self-framing, in which Pepys, as the desirable male, bursts upon the screen and pursues the woman down an alleyway, doused no doubt in some expensive perfume. But then Pepys is an exhibitionist; he likes to boast of his sexual adventures and write them up in their vainglorious splendour. A new sexual conquest is as newsworthy as a report on international politics. After a while we become accustomed to him breaking off from a report on sunken ships to list the daily beatitudes of sexual pleasures with maidservants and the sight of himself in a new waistcoat.[223]

This is hardly surprising: diaries foster obsessions, moments when the brain splits off from public affairs and skedaddles back to its private concerns. Sex, of course, is one of these, and in this regard Pepys's diary is something like his private closet where he stores matters on his mind and in his heart. In the middle of the Second Anglo-Dutch War, when England's naval base at Chatham is under heavy attack, Pepys is found discussing the matter of the King's mistresses with his colleague Mr Povey and by what means these women are brought into the royal chambers. Somehow, the sexual activities of the King and his brother, the Duke of York, are woven into a larger state canvas, which links the royal bed partners to 'the family['s] horrible disorder of being in debt'.[224] As we have already ascertained, Pepys is as interested in domestic matters as anything, and this includes household finances and sexual contentment. In conversation, he moves between chamber and closet, gliding through the private spaces of seventeenth-century domestic life as easily as a household servant.[225]

Metaphorically speaking, his diary does the same: it roams like a private eye from one chamber to the next, bringing back intimate findings. Pepys knows how to foster social intimacy. Indeed, he has a special talent for it. An important part of his reportage is a list of growing attachments. Most crucially, there is his employer, the Earl of Sandwich, who by October 1662 is calling him into his chamber for 'private discourse' on 'jealousys' of the court, which includes the Duke of Albemarle's cruel treatment of a 'company of poor wretches' he has dragged up and down the streets.[226] And as is expected of him, Pepys lends his disapproving ears.

Many of his attachments are formed in coffee shops and taverns, seventeenth-century spaces of male intimacy and bonding. Sitting in the King's Head at Charing Cross he hears the whispered opinions of his colleague Creed on the matter of the 'young Crofts' (James Scott, Duke of Monmouth), who, so Creed tells him, is the lawful son of the King Charles II. Monmouth is the most contentious figure of the era. By 1685 his presence is a real threat to the reigning King, James II. Monmouth is emerging as the crown's usurper. Idle tavern chatter, then, is quickly turning into substantial history. Pepys and Creed are in fact musing on the real future of the English monarchy. Will he or won't he topple the crown?

*

Scandal begins at the top, with royalty. In Britain, the scandal sheet emerged in the seventeenth century with the figure of the pamphleteer, the likes of indefatigable Nathaniel Butter whose Weekly News was a constant source of irritation to the Jacobean and Caroline establishment.[227] But 'scandal' is first coined in English during the late period of Elizabeth's reign, the 1590s, when contests between favoured courtiers – the infamous Essex–Cecil row, for example – were hot news.[228] In Elizabeth's court, reputations were always hovering on a precarious line and paranoia easily festered.

'Scandal', from the Greek 'skandalon', refers to inflammatory information which, if released, might 'trap' or 'snare' an individual, causing him to fall or stumble. Elizabethan court poet, Thomas Wyatt, obliquely referring to his affair with Anne Boleyn, conjures scandal in the figure of a naked foot 'stalking' in his chamber. An intercepted diary is something like one of Wyatt's loose feet: a piece of flesh left dangerously dangling. If one has something to hide, a diary surely would be the place to look. Pepys knew this and so hid his diaries away in his personal library.

Still, there is a thin veil between news and gossip. As all tabloid editors know, it is easy to legitimise the pernicious effects of gossip by assigning it to the category of 'newsworthy'. By the eighteenth century, local gossip in London was beginning to sell. The *Tatler*, begun in 1709 under the editorship of Richard Steele, managed to convert gossip into a recognisable form of social criticism. 'Tattle' is idle chat among women, and the purpose of the *Tatler*, so Steele declared, was to provide the fairer sex with the opportunity to hear tales told about town.[229] We read the diaries of others surely because it satisfies a baser instinct, to poke and pry and tell tales.

Telling Lies

Woolf's London diary is full of tittle-tattle, or, put more frankly, 'lies'. There is nothing socially improving about Woolf's need to fictionalise herself; it is merely literary self-indulgence. Her diary eggs her on. 'I was telling lies to Dorothy Bussy the other day about this very book – how I lived in writing – & wrote & wrote in the streets – & coming home floated it off here,' she writes in June 1922.[230] Specifically, Woolf is telling lies about her diary, fictionalising the nature of her relationship with her 'book' as a teenage girl might spice up the story of a romance to a friend.

The juvenile in Woolf wants to impress Dorothy, and so her pen 'floats' on towards more talk and more affairs. Moments later, she turns to the matter of her acquaintance Ralph Partridge and his affair with Valentine Dobrée. Here is another piece of real life rapidly turning into fiction. Ralph, a recent guest of the Woolfs, is in love and behaving badly. Woolf notes that he is something resembling a 'mad bull'. But Ralph has been deceived. While he has been carrying on with Valentine, his partner, the painter Dora Carrington, has been involved with Gerald Brenan. And so goes the topsy-turvy world of a Bloomsbury-style romance, whose convoluted affairs, the editor of Woolf's diary tells us, might be unpicked by a diligent reading of the letters and diaries of Carrington and the Personal Record of Gerald Brenan.[231]

Affairs are complicated things and not for the simple-minded. They need some tracing and an awful lot of arranging. Woolf responds to Ralph with a declaration: she could fill a book with her opinions on love, and perhaps will. This 'ordinary Englishman' in love is full of 'stupidity, blindness, callousness', behaviours far outweighing the 'magic virtues of passion'. Woolf listens to Ralph's story of betrayal and partly believes him. But she is quick to note his flimsy self-disguise. Ralph is not as honest as he might think. Like Carrington he has also told lies, 'concealed essentials'. Woolf undertakes a complicated bit of emotional detective work. She sits back and assesses the bluffs and double-bluffs of a man in love who has both betrayed and been betrayed.

The story continues in public. Travelling back together from a lecture, Woolf finally strikes out at the besotted Ralph: 'I should have left you if you had treated me like that,' she bellows at him across the railway carriage. Ralph, she realises is 'a bit of a maniac' in love. Suddenly the maniac's eyes turn on her, 'rose pink', the colour of foxes. Woolf in the role of pursued 'rabbit', shouts 'louder and louder', scandalising the fellow passengers, we imagine.

Woolf closes the episode with a summary of the affair, including her own involvement in its framing. Her entry sensibly omits details, partly to save time, but also partly out of 'discretion'. With a journalist's sense of an afterlife, her own but also Ralph's and Carrington's, she censors her story in order to leave out 'the links' as she calls them: names and places that might assign blame. She does, however, draw a philosophical conclusion: lovers, she notes, like to travel along 'convenient railway lines of convention'. They create a recognisable story of themselves in love through which they can hastily 'speed' towards their 'lusts' without any question of consequences.

This is the thrilling ride of romance. We think of Sylvia Plath speeding towards Paris in the hope of reuniting with her old flame, Richard Sassoon. Carrington, Woolf suspects, is in it only for the ride. She is in love with no one, and this fact, which Ralph surely suspects too, spurs him on to new conquests.[232] Woolf is describing potential scandal from a journalist's point of view. Certainly she has an eye on posterity, but she is also, in this case, hearing the news of Ralph's affair with a biographer's ear. What might biographers say? What would the future Virginia Woolf say?

Virginia Woolf and Incest in the Brighton Public Library

I discovered Virginia Woolf's diaries on the floor of Brighton town library. I was fifteen, nearly sixteen, and I had just left home to come and live in East Sussex. I was in Woolf's county, the county of Rodmell and Glynde, of Lewes and Charleston Farmhouse; places patterned with footpaths and fields, places leading to poppies and the sea.

But Woolf's Sussex was not my version of Sussex. My Sussex was owned by West Sussex County Council on the other side of the county line, somewhere between Portslade and Shoreham-by-Sea, somewhere near a power station filled with asbestos that was later blown up because it killed several seagulls and sailors. My restless Cassandra Mortmain had managed to run away. She'd acquired a social worker and a Special File. She'd left her damp house by the sea.

The first thing I knew about Virginia Woolf was that she might have been sexually abused. A woman called Louise

DeSalvo told me this. Louise DeSalvo's book was only concerned with Virginia Woolf's relationship to sex. According to
Louise DeSalvo it was sex that had turned her mad; it was sex
that turned all women mad.

But Virginia Woolf didn't seem very bothered about sex, I
thought, as I ploughed through her five volumes of diaries on
the public library shelves. I pushed Louise DeSalvo's garish
book away (the cover was a violent purple or pink to match),
and hid it at the back of the shelves. I didn't want anyone else
to find it. Louise DeSalvo was making me feel sick. Besides,
it was silly. Madness and incest and sexual abuse: these were
the sorts of things you might find written in the file of a young
girl in care.

Virginia Woolf didn't write about sex. Let's just say it
wasn't top of her agenda. She wrote about people glimmering
and gleaming at parties, sparkling people; people so clever and
witty she just had to write it all down. She wrote about the war
coming on, about her latest novel, about her fear of not being
as good as Katherine Mansfield, her main rival (who perhaps
fortunately for Woolf died young). She wrote about the views
from her London and Sussex homes, she wrote about her
servants; she wrote about writing and writers, but most of all
she wrote an awful lot about reading: books and books and
books – the whole of Samuel Pepys when she was fifteen or
sixteen. No. Virginia Woolf didn't have time for sex. And just
because someone might have looked up her skirt or down her
dress when she was sixteen didn't mean you had to put it in
her file. These sorts of things happened to girls all the time.
They happened to Cassandra Mortmain's sister, Rose, who
gets kissed an awful lot – and then the rest.

When I first found Virginia Woolf's diaries I couldn't put
them down. And it wasn't because of the sex. It was because I

had found a voice that was as strong and still and distilled as anyone's I'd ever heard. It was a voice that passed opinion undilutedly. And unlike my aunt, Virginia Woolf did know what she was talking about; really knew, as opposed to just sounding like she knew. She'd done the reading and the research. She'd been to the library. She'd bought her journal-notebook. I opened the first page of her first diary and read the first sentence: 'While waiting to buy a book in which to record my impressions first of Christina Rossetti, then of Byron, I had better write them here.' Some time in the winter of 1987 in Brighton Public Library I wrote that sentence down.

*

Pepys certainly never expected anyone to read his diary but the fear of a reader surely led him to write in a macaronic tongue of French-Spanish-Italian. Perhaps diaries, as Susan Sontag suggests, elicit attention; they ask to be read. It might also be that in the careful diary code Pepys constructed for himself he hid away from his own conscience, mitigated the effects of his sexual shenanigans. So frank is his statement of shame when he is discovered by his wife with his hand up Deb Willet's skirt, that it is impossible to imagine anyone but himself listening in. In front of his diary, Pepys is a contrite child left with a feeling of 'the greatest sorrow' he has ever known 'in this world'. His confession is childish, swaddled in a lover's baby-speak: 'I was with my main in her cunny.'

The make-up scene is equally childish; there is a lot of shouting on the part of Pepys's wife, Elizabeth, delightfully described by Pepys as his wife's voice 'com[ing] to her'. And then in the midst of this there is a sudden and dramatic confession that she has turned Roman Catholic.[233] This is a smart tactic on the part of Mrs Pepys, as her threat of apostasy pushes Pepys to hastily renew his marital vows. Catholicism, always the more dangerous choice of religion in seventeenth-century England (even if the King himself was a private adherent), coupled with sex, is a powder keg about to explode.

But sex doesn't go away that easily. Pepys keeps at it, even on Sundays, and in a way his diary gives him licence – so certain is he that it will remain private. During another night of ranting, Mrs Pepys threatens to make public her husband's 'shame'. There is nothing left but to grovel, and so the long-winded domestic pantomime ends with Pepys, in the role of reformed knight, pledging love and allegiance to his wife. October 1668 closes with a rather shameful totting up of his list of follies and a further reckoning with his conscience.[234]

At crisis point, Pepys is forced to make his affair with Deb 'privy' to another, and calls upon his loyal clerk Will Hewer to act as diplomat and go-between until a final resolution is made. Pepys, under orders from his wife, agrees to write to Deb and name her a 'whore', swearing never to see her again. Will makes sure the letter is never delivered, but peace is made between husband and wife, and Pepys sets down a promise, a renewal of his marital vows almost, in his diary: 'But by the grace of God, though I love the poor girl and wish her well, as having gone too far toward the undoing of her, yet I will never enquire after her or think of her more – my peace being certainly to do right to my wife.'[235]

In some sense Pepys's oath adheres to the original purpose of the spiritual diary: as a means of renewing one's covenant with God. He isn't directly renewing vows with God – it is his wife to whom he is most answerable – but 'God' is certainly a stand-in for his conscience. His 'mauvais amours' must come to an end.[236]

Reading about Pepys's sorry affair we suspect that diaries might in fact encourage the adolescent in those who keep them; foster the fantasy and thrill of that first, heady love. If Pepys's diary is partly responsible for his regression or deviances, he now relies upon it to make him a new man. Here is the other side of the Puritan journal: a document that can stand as loyal witness to an individual's self-renewal and spiritual clean-up.

Fortunately for him, Pepys's affair with Deb doesn't get out and the whole business, as far as we know, is contained within the inner circle of his household. Pepys has a lucky escape from scandal; his wife stays mum and so does his diary, which remains locked away in his personal library until the first edition appears in 1825, well over 100 years after his death. We can only assume that Pepys manages to 'wear Deb out of [his] mind'.[237] Dalliances after Deb remain mostly theoretical, and because there is no hope of an elopement, there is no afterlife to this story. With his eyes failing, his diary fails too, and so any hope of a place for storing the history of his 'amours'.[238]

*

Diaries are often archives of secret love-lives, some abortive, others consummated. Some 140 years on from Pepys's broken relationship with Deb Willet, one of the great elopements of literary history is recorded quietly inside a shared journal. On July 28th 1814 Mary Godwin – daughter of Mary Wollstonecraft and William Godwin – and Percy Bysshe Shelley arrange to meet on the corner of the City of London's Hatton Garden to set sail for France. Mary and Shelley carry on where Pepys and Deb left off. They leave behind an outraged Mr and Mrs Godwin and a distraught Harriet Shelley, Shelley's wife, whose abandonment is barely mentioned. The episode is noted in their shared journal:

England – 1814
July 28. The night preceding this morning, all being decided – I ordered a chaise to be ready by 4 o clock. I watched until the lightning & the stars became pale. At length it was 4. I believed it not possible that we should succeed: still there appeared to lurk some danger even in certainty. I went. I saw her. She came to me. Yet one quarter of an hour remained. Still some arrangements must be made, & she left me for a short time. How dreadful did this time appear. It seemed that we trifled with life & hope. a few minutes past she was in my arms – we were safe. We were on our road to Dover.[239]

Gauche, awkward, uncomfortable and ill-thought-out by moonlight, this is teenage gothic. It is not too far removed from the recent *Twilight* series, whose aesthetic is something like the silent films of the twenties, filled with the self-conscious stammers and pauses of American teenagers trying to play it cool: all grimaces and grins and few words. Time and space are all theirs, but they are poorly handled and little understood. Nothing is suave or sophisticated because there really isn't much of a plot; not much has been planned – only the leaving. At nineteen, Shelley seems to lack the confidence or aplomb to pull it off. Despite himself, he does it anyway, in the way teenagers do – without really knowing how or why. There is a plan, but it's rather shoddy. Resistance is inevitable; someone will pursue them, as Mrs Godwin, Mary's stepmother, does. But that is all part of the teenage thrill.

The entry continues with a description of the lovers' crossing to Calais, where the stormy crossing stands in for a night of passion. Shelley focuses on the poetry of the event, filmic atmosphere rather than action. Intimacy – at sea, and during a storm – doesn't get much more exciting. All the heady anticipation of leaving is consummated in the crossing. Finally, the young lovers have a plot:

> The evening was most beautiful. The sand slowly receded. We felt secure. There was little wind – the sails flapped in the flagging breeze. The moon rose, the night came on, & with the night a slow heavy swell and a fresher breeze which soon became so violent as to toss the boat very much … Mary was much affected by the sea. She could scarcely move. She lay in my arms thro the night, the little strength which remained to my own exhausted frame was all expended in keeping her head in rest on my bosom. The wind was violent & contrary. If we could not reach Calais the sailors proposed making for Boulogne. They promised only two hours sail from the shore, yet hour after hour past & we were still far distant when the moon sunk in the red & stormy horizon, & the fast flashing lightning became pale in the breaking day.[240]

Drama intensifies with the prospect of death. Shelley's teenage fanaticism, the all-or-nothing of young love, declares union in death to be better than separation in life. The passage follows the timing of sexual passion run through the course of the storm. Conditions, at first, are perfect for love-making. The sea is a smooth bed; a warm breeze wafts across the prostrate lovers. And then the moon comes up. Passion intensifies as the breeze turns into a strong, whipping wind. It is too much for Mary who becomes sick.

But the storm abates and passion subsides: 'suddenly the broad sun rose over France'. Here is a sort of post-coital calm, through which a tiny peep from Mary is at last heard: 'Mary was there. Shelley was also with me.' Sealed safe within their love-contract, the lovers dismiss with comic presumption and arrogance the negative effects of their elopement – the inconvenienced adult world: 'In the evening Captain Davison came & told us that a fat lady had arrived, who had said th[at] I had run away with her daughter.'[241] Teenage self-conviction quickly dismisses any reality that might challenge or thwart their own. Parents and dependants are inconvenient appendages.

The Shelleys' shared journal encourages an exclusive view of the world in which the journal plays co-conspirator to the plotless contingencies of teenage love. The journal ruthlessly ignores anything extraneous or indeed any impediment to love. Potentially, this includes the wraith-like figure of Claire Clairmont, the couple's seventeen-year-old travelling companion and co-conspirator, who barely appears in his fiction but is presumably there throughout the entire tour. Claire is the third eye and party to the affair and it is perhaps in imitation of Mary and Shelley that she begins her own passionate affair with Lord Byron in the spring of 1816. She is ripe and ready for such an adventure and needs only the smallest of encouragements: Byron's admiring overtures to her stepfather, Godwin, are enough to set her writing to the philandering lord.[242]

Beneath the shadow of the Shelley affair another scandal was brewing. The affair with Byron left Claire pregnant; her daughter Allegra Clairmont was born in January 1817 in the wake of familial tragedy. A month earlier, on December 10th, the body of young Harriet Shelley was discovered in the Serpentine. Harriet had drowned herself. Two months prior to this, Fanny Imlay Godwin, daughter of Godwin's first wife

Mary Wollstonecraft, committed suicide, aged twenty-two.[243]

The published version of the Shelleys' diary omits any sense of the real-life costs of their elopement. In what became *History of a Six Week Tour* (1818), the elopement is entirely concealed, as is the process of collaborative authorship. In the public eye, propriety takes precedence. The folly of young love is tided away into an 'improving' travel narrative penned by Mary, which is in fact her writing debut. But the History doesn't tell the whole truth. Percy Shelley's voice is no longer heard; instead, he and Claire are folded away into the role of 'companions'.[245] Percy Bysshe Shelley, the journal vows, was never ever there.

*

Gossip destroys the bridge between public and private matter; it devalues the notion of the inward and ineffable. In the ugly face of gossip, nothing is left unheard or unsaid and it was for these reasons that philosopher Soren Kierkegaard despised it. Scandal and gossip also ruin lives. 'I forgot that every little action of the common day makes or unmakes character, and that therefore what one has done in the secret chamber one has some day to cry aloud on the housetop,' writes Oscar Wilde in his 50,000-word letter 'from the depths', addressed to his former lover, Lord Alfred Douglas.[245] Written between January and March 1897 while Wilde was imprisoned in Reading Gaol, his heart-rending *De Profundis* was never posted – prison authorities forbade him from sending it – and so Wilde carried the manuscript out of prison with him a month later.

De Profundis is an extended, heartfelt response to the devastation of scandal, and although it was conceived as a letter, it has all the qualities of confession and contrition of a spiritual journal. It is the case of a despairing man finding expression. In a letter to his friend and literary executor, Robert Ross (the man charged to deliver his letter to Lord Alfred), Wilde states the case quite clearly: 'mere expression is to an artist the supreme and only form of life.'[246] A life without writing was, for Wilde, no life at all.

Bound to the rigid routine of prison life, the incarcerated writer finds relief from the flow of ink across paper. But Wilde's access to the time and resources for writing was tightly controlled. He was permitted only one page of blue regulation prison paper at a time and he was never allowed to keep the fruits of his labours, the page being taken away at the end of each day. Such mean restrictions make De Profundis an exercise in careful self-control, since Wilde could not spill over.

Posted only after he left prison, Wilde's harrowing 50,000-word letter turns into an address to himself, and a means of repairing his reputation in his own eyes. Perhaps in sympathy with this, Ross heavily expurgated the first printed edition. No direct mention of Lord Alfred was to appear, and, in the end, Ross did not follow Wilde's directions: he made two copies, as asked, but he kept the original himself. It was a copy that was sent to Douglas, whose receipt Douglas never acknowledged.

Ross's decision was canny. Unsurprisingly, sales of De Profundis were phenomenal. Between 1905 and 1913 De Profundis went through 28 editions, of which the first edition alone sold 10,000.[247] Wilde's literary reputation soared, proving that scandal can also make lives.

Wilde's particular problem was his incautious life as a homo-sexual and his taste for the theatrical. Events turned public with Wilde's decision to sue his lover's father, the Marquess of Queensberry. The prompt was a provocative calling card, left for Wilde by the fuming marquess with the now infamous inscription: 'For Oscar Wilde posing as a Somdomite'. The upshot was a messy court-brawl in which all the salacious details of Wilde's associations with blackmailers, male prosti-tutes, cross-dressers and homosexual brothels were wrung out. Wilde lost the fight and with it all his privacy and freedom. The price he paid for his fit of pique was high. In *De Profundis* he records what he calls his one long moment of suffering:

All this took place in the early part of November of the year before last. A great river of life flows between you and a date so distant. Hardly, if at all, can you see across so wide a waste ... Suffering is one long moment. We cannot divide it by seasons. We can only record its moods, and chronicle their return ... The paralysing immobility of a life, every circumstance of which is regulated after an unchangeable pattern, so that eat and drink and walk and lie down and pray, or kneel at least for prayer, according to the inflexible laws of an iron formula – this immobile quality, that makes each dreadful day in the very minutest detail like its brother ... For us, there is only the season of sorrow. The very sun and moon seem taken from us. Outside, the day maybe blue and gold, but the light that creeps down from the thickly-muffled glass of the small iron barred window beneath which one sits is grey and niggard. It is always twilight in one's cell, as it is always twilight in one's heart.[248]

Colwood Adolescent Unit,
Some Time in the 1980s

One day in November I was sent to Colwood Adolescent Unit, a place with bars on the windows and lights out at nine. Men in white uniforms came to take me. When I saw their faces coming towards me, so serious and still, I thought they were ghosts coming back from the dead. I screamed. The only sound they made was the sound of plastic swishing around their feet. The sound of plastic usually meant the end of clothes, the end of privacy. It meant the beginning of draughts and cold feet, the beginning of prodding and poking and peering.

As the men in uniform shuffled about by my bed, I scrabbled around for my diary, my life on paper, the place where I could think and breathe. For a year or more I had been only a series of notes in medical books: the private scribblings of Dr Mougne, Consultant Psychiatrist; Carolyn Taylor, Social Worker; Dr Latham, GP; the Art Therapist, Linda; the Man on the Moon peering down with his telescope. Whoever had wanted to prod and poke and peer had, then written it down in their notebook and locked it away in their desk. I was a file and a folder, a series of Strictly Confidentials tied up in red tape. I'd been strangled.

Late at night lying in the beds without springs, the beds without soft parts, the beds without a soul (we were moved every so often so we didn't feel too much at home), I felt around for my journal and pulled it towards me. I clung to it like a life-raft. Nobody should know about this but me. Nobody should get inside, under its skin. They would only misinterpret and misread, all those people with degrees in psychiatry and psychology, social work and therapy, listening and healing and imagining what-not. None of them knew about me. What is more, I wouldn't let them.

That night I decided to start writing in code. I would write poems in my journal, my poems and the poems of other poets. After all, nobody really understood what was going on in poetry – not really – not even those who wrote it. Poetry just came suddenly, out of nowhere. Sometimes it spoke the truth, but often it just spoke riddles. I would speak in riddles too, like the Sphinx at Giza. I would flummox them all. When they read my journal they would throw their hands in the air and despair. Like Oscar Wilde, I would would turn myself to stone. 'Prison life makes one see people and things as they are really are. That is why it turns one to stone' (Oscar Wilde, letter to Robert Ross).[249]

Putting Yourself Out There

The diary has come a long way from Pepys's discreetly coded manuscripts. The traditional diary or journal has been replaced by its online version, the blog. Blogs are run-away creatures. In the blogosphere, you can type endlessly away into a blank universe, into a companionable silence. You imagine an audience, but it remains anonymous. In the blogosphere you are in the exclusive company of 'I' and 'me'.

Facebook, Twitter and the culture of blogging emerge from a celebrity culture whose central premise is that anyone, and indeed all of us, is intrinsically interesting. Twitter gets you followers, Facebook finds you friends. In the world of social networking we are all celebrities, although only some of us really are. Stephen Fry was one of the first British celebrities to draw attention to the Twitter phenomenon, with his by now notorious Twitter or 'tweet' update while stuck in a lift: 'Ok. This is now mad. I am stuck in a lift on the 26th floor of Centre Point. Hell's teeth. We could be here for hours. Arse, poo, and widdle. (2.47pm, Feb 3rd, 2009 via Twitter for iPhone).'[250]

A form of micro-blogging and social networking via text message, Twitter is for a generation of compulsive communicators unable to stand still. Footloose and fancy-free, twittering is for those on the move, and as Stephen Fry demonstrates, it is a good way of coping with that most frustrating of contemporary experiences: not being able to move.

Tweeting is quick, airy movement. An instant reflex, a flick-of-the-wrist approach to communication, tweeting is a sort of premature mental ejaculation. Listen to Lady Gaga tweeting after an interview with Howard Stern: 'Just left @HowardStern, rockers with long hair have a sweetspot for girls like me. He was a doll.'[251] This is blatant self-promotion, or, you could say, out-and-out self-creation. Lady Gaga is writing her own fan mail at the same time as she is creating an image. Gaga is pleased to note that Howard Stern, the most disreputable of talk show chauvinists, thinks she's all right. He may even fancy her a bit. Whatever the case, Gaga is swirling happily about in a micro-celebrity climate of her own making.

But I might be wrong about this. I'm new to tweeting. Perhaps a tweet is a more reflective form of thinking. A friend of mine tells me that people can spend hours creating a tweet. A tweet is a form of haiku in which every syllable, every one of your 140 characters counts. A tweet is not just another bit of noise floating through the cyber-universe. It is a brief meditation on the universe. On Twitter you can say something philosophical about Jeremy Corbyn refusing to sing the

National Anthem, the return of socialism, Obama's decision to bomb Syria. You can comment on the state of the nation and the globe. What is more, people will listen. Their attention spans won't run out. They might even quote back or recycle what you say. That's called retweeting.

Still, I find it hard not to think of Twitter as just another form of social gossip, a quick blurt. One moment you tweet about a celebrity break-up and the next you tweet about your own. Certainly, Twitter marks the end of bounded public and private worlds. The traditionally private world, the sphere of the household – Pepys in bed with Elizabeth giving her a black eye – has no separate form of life from the Pepys strutting about around Whitehall.[252] Private or casual modes of communicating have not only engulfed our public world, they produce it.

The Plot on Paper

A decade before his death, having fallen from the pinnacle of his administrative power, Pepys was considering the condition of his personal estate on paper; he was rereading his diary and deciding what to do with it. Should he or shouldn't he keep this 'tumultuous' mass of papers as he described his diary obliquely to his friend Thomas Gale?[253] Would this mass of papers turn, posthumously, against him?

Thankfully, Pepys decided to keep his six-volume diary, replacing the books on his library shelves and reordering his catalogue to accommodate their presence.[254] Posterity was paramount to Pepys's sense of self. Posterity, he knew, could be guaranteed with a book.[255] Pepys must have carefully considered the content of his diary and decided it contained enough good material to deserve being kept. His diary, he believed, would make a good book.

Pepys's decision would surely have been quite different today. In our contemporary world of viral information leaks, Pepys's sex life would have brought a newspaper – perhaps several – a big, juicy story. We live in an age of unclassified information; a titbit of information can now be spread across the internet in a matter of seconds. Reputations rise and fall in a day, half a day, an hour even. Our understanding of time is now almost entirely related to the spread of news, most of it negative. Scandal is everyday and mainstream. In the face of a widespread internet culture, the preservation of individual reputation is now a major cultural, that is to say legislative, concern.[256]

Diary-time marks an older and more sacred experience of time. Before the explosion of internet culture, privacy could be found by simply withdrawing from the public eye: in the mode of Pepys withdrawing to his chamber and Woolf retiring to her Sussex home. Privacy was a matter of decorum, self-determined and self-selected, above all expected, a normal part of self-regulation. In an age of practically universal web access, the diary represents an old-fashioned sense of self-scrutiny and surveillance, a period of personal introspection.

Our culture expects us all to be blurters and self-promoters. The desire for privacy is something we now label deviant, antisocial. To be part of an online global village is surely what we all want; to take ourselves off a professional webpage is surely the road to professional ruin? Privacy is a privilege few of us can now afford.[257]

*

The right to privacy, defined in American terms as 'the right to be left alone', is in substance, on legal paper and in tort-talk, crumbly and ineffective. It amounts to little more than, as contemporary novelist Jonathan Franzen puts it, a 'Cheshire cat of values', nothing more than a 'winning smile' or a polite glance back at classic liberal notions of individual liberty.[258] The end of traditional diary-keeping – a life led on paper not on screen – signals the end of a certain kind of relationship with our private life.

We live, more and more, in a paperless world, a culture in which private lives and private thoughts lack material, bodily weight. On a recent visit to a stationer, I was struck again by the fashionable return of the beautiful journal and notebook. Diaries and journals have made a return. I picked up one after another shiny, glossy, patterned and embossed beautiful book-object, books that felt and looked like jewellery, books I wanted to put inside my bag. In the modern world, there is nothing that is not an object for our craving.

Woolf was a great shopper for notebooks. So many of her diary entries mention a trip to buy a new notebook. On March 29th 1940, a year before her death, she is still planning her choreography of London around buying a notebook. 'The river. Say the Thames at London Bridge; & buying a note-book.'[259] Rivers and writing merge: the body of the great writer in the Ouse and the great body on paper left behind.

Paper has its own texture and consciousness, its own countable and accountable units: the page. The diaries of Pepys and Woolf are impressive precisely because of their vast numbers of pages, their bulk. Turning those pages we experience a modicum, a small portion, of the weight of hours spent writing. Woolf measured her life in paper – 26 volumes – and Pepys did the same. Pepys took his diary life very seriously:

all six volumes of his diary were finely bound, an indication surely of how he valued his diary life.[260] As we have already determined, both wished for afterlives. Neither wished to be forgotten.

*

Diaries prompt self-reassessment, the opportunity for a second look at yourself. A diary perhaps promises to retell, to those who read them, the life story of their writer: what Horatio promises to Hamlet at the moment of his dying.[261] The tragedy of the diary form, if we can call it that, is the near-miss reality of the event in the first place. What the diary longs for is a true realisation of the moment, a moment of fully flushed, fully present consciousness. As a writer, the realisation of this moment was Woolf's life-long quest. She knew that a diary cannot ever compete with life; it can only try to comment on it.

A diary may help you know yourself better, certainly it will help others know you better, but can a diary help anyone change for the better? A diary cannot work miracles of self-transformation. Pepys knew this when he recorded, for the umpteenth time, his exploits with Deb Willet. Keeping a diary was not going to stop Pepys from fooling around. What it could do was lend a shape to his day. His diary provided a central structure and from this, the recorded structure of the day, he might better reflect upon his opinion of himself and others.

If, ultimately, the diary is a form of conversation with yourself away from the world – a verbal 'finger exercise', as Woolf describes it – then it must also have some beneficial effect on our relations to the world when we return to it.[262] In a world where rapid response seems to be more valued than reflection, the diary might be just the sort of daily exercise we need to draw us back into a richer present. Perhaps we would all be happier if we sought out a little time and space for our inner Pepys. If we went to our chamber once a day to scribble down our thoughts on the day. If we stopped browsing, pausing, surfing and tweeting and began really looking around us, at the small Very Important Things.[263] Who knows, the next day might even go better.

THE DIARY AFTERLIFE

Those films from our Orkney family holiday make my brother cry, so we've stopped playing them. Now they lie under my bed gathering dust. When I lie down on the floor sideways I can see my mother's long thin handwriting reaching upwards, her thin calligraphy marking out the dates of each videotape, her ornate blue handwriting running along the length of glossy plastic spines and I wonder how it is that my mother's handwriting has survived.

She must have used a special pen, a waterproof pen. My mother was very good at knowing which pens to use on which surface. She knew the difference between a permanent and an impermanent mark. She knew which would wash away and which would stay.

*

In Orcadia I disappeared. I vanished inside the sea and sky. In the end, I think it was the sky that took me. I lay on the ground outside our motel with my diary pressed beneath me to stop it blowing away. I lay outside there for days looking up at the grey sky getting nearer and nearer.

On either side I could hear the sound of children, other

children, not my relatives, but children speaking strange, slurring words. Children with orange hair and strange words in their mouth came near me but I turned away. I wanted to write in my diary; I didn't want to say hello. I was here on holiday; why wouldn't they leave me alone? I didn't want to be an Orcadian. I couldn't be an Orcadian. I didn't understand a word they said, I didn't want to know any more children; there were already too many children following me around. When they asked me to come and play with them I said 'no'. I'd never done that before. I wrote 'no' in my diary. 'No, no, no.'

*

One day my mum came outside to tell me that we were going to Skara Brae, the reason we had come here, why we were staying in a motel at the edge of the world. Skara Brae was the beginning of everything, the place where women first began. My aunt didn't seem to care about the men. We had come to Skara Brae to find the bodies of our ancestors. They were all women.

But my aunt's tapes are all that is left of that holiday; there is nothing else, and the story on tape is this: in front of the low stone walls, the flat, wide sheep with indifferent stares, in front of the bumpy hillocks running down to the sea, there are always four or five or six skinny little boys, aged six or seven or eight; skinny boys dressed in combat trousers and drainpipe jeans topped with Aran jumpers. Pale little worms rising up from the ground, little boys 'playing the fool', as my mother always said of them, against a background of sober history; a landscape of deep, quiet ritual. Little boys jumping up and down on green mounds, on top of hours and hours of sorting of utensils and whittling away at wood; hours and hours of rubbing and chaffing and winding and wrapping and digging, pummelling and pulling, scoring and boring small threads of tough plant tendrils through narrow slits in wood. Little boys stamping and leaping on top of women's hands, women's fingers, women's skin, fastening themselves to wooden utensils, women's hands tying utensils to string, string torn from berry plants, string knitted from thick grasses, string that hung their beads from their necks before one day a large wind whipped up a foul temper and sent the sea over the top of the low stone walls and washed all the women away.

*

I don't have my diary from that time any more, but I wish, I most bitterly wish that I did. I would like to have known if I could spell Skara Brae, aged twelve, nearly thirteen. Did I spell it 'Skara Bray' or 'Scara Bray'? I can hear my aunt saying those words. They were her words. When she said Skara Brae it sounded like an old dead donkey. But Skara Brae was a Neolithic (could I spell that aged twelve?) dwelling, an ancient settlement, a ring of stone houses with sitting rooms and living rooms and bedrooms, with small shelves for storing wooden toys.

Skara Brae looked like the farmyard set with stone walls we played with back home. Little grass patches sat on top of the stone all sorted into neat boxes. Inside the stone boxes were more stones where people sat. People at Skara Brae were all women, so my aunt said, women who left their beads behind. Or at least one did. The only evidence of human life left behind on Skara Brae was a set of beads. I wondered if the women of Skara Brae used their beads to count the days, and whether they counted forward or backward.

*

In 1972, the year I was born, archaeologists dug up a handle made from willow and a rope made from crowberries. I had no idea how a rope could be made from berries, but my grandmother explained that it was the plant that made the rope. I wish I had found a piece of rope from Skara Brae but I don't think we were allowed to touch much. The only ropes were the ones keeping children out, like sheep from their pens. If we strayed too close to the small stone boxes sheepdogs were set on us.

I walked around the desolate stone boxes covered with grass and felt as though I were inside a tomb. This is what it must feel like after you're dead and buried, I thought; to have the sky pressing down overhead and the sea so far from view that you could no longer hear it. I walked along the edge of the stone walls and realised that the wind had disappeared; the wind had stopped. Behind the stone walls everything was still. Nothing moved. Nobody breathed.

I wanted something I could hold, something I could take away with me, something I could put in my diary. I looked down at the ground for a souvenir and saw only small grey stones. Stones were everywhere; there were too many stones. I wanted to press a dark crowberry between the white pages, to feel something alive between my fingers. I wanted to make something, squash and push and press like the women of Skara Brae. I wanted to crush out the colour and store it away. Crowberries, I thought, must look like the beady eyes of the crow: dark and mysterious and cruel. I wanted to be frightened when I opened up the pages of my diary, after I got back home. I wanted something to peer at, something to bring this place back to life, something to bring me back to life after the holiday was over.

But I found nothing on the ground at Skara Brae, and when I looked up I only saw my aunt with her camera pointing towards me, her dark beady eye swallowing me up. I saw only the small black box of the video camera moving silently across the grey sea. I felt for my diary in the breast pocket of my blue jumpsuit but my pocket was empty. Behind that pocket there was nothing but bones.

Diary Survival

Diaries have a long legacy of aiding and abetting survival. Daniel Defoe's *Robinson Crusoe* (1719) is a story of survival by diary writing. Shipwrecked upon an 'Island of Despair', Defoe's hero is forced into emergency thinking. He begins a journal as a way of ordering his desperate and diminished reality; and so the journal becomes a log book of the place in which he finds himself, a list of nouns that read as objects: 'the Shore', 'my Habitation', 'an Attack', 'proper Place', 'Rock', 'Wall', 'Piles', 'Cables' and 'Turf'. Among these is 'all Day' and 'Night', the basic units of diurnal reality, whose distinction is essential for sanity and survival.

Journal writing is an essential part of Crusoe's survival plan; by making himself accountable to his journal, Crusoe conjures another body to haul him through the day. Crusoe curtails his journal as he starts to run out of paper and ink. As the journal nears extinction, as the paper runs out, so the recorded contents, the daily supply of events, dwindle. Crusoe survives but the journal does not. With the appearance of Man Friday, Defoe gains another body; in Friday his journal becomes incarnate.

Defoe's story highlights the importance of the diary as a

physical object; its presence as a near-holy thing in the lives of those who keep them. Raised within a culture of Protestant dissent, Defoe was naturally aware of the significance of diaries as tools for private spiritual practice.[264] But diaries, as Defoe makes explicit in his famous novel, are more than a means of sustaining a spiritual commitment: they offer material weight and comfort, paper and ink, perhaps a leather binding or soft cover: the texture and substance indicative of the life held within.

*

The most devoted of teenage diarists, Anne Frank, placed her diary among her most essential living belongings: 'The first thing I put in was this diary, then hair curlers, handkerchiefs, schoolbooks, a comb, old letters; I put in the craziest things with the idea that we were going into hiding. But I'm not sorry, memories mean more to me than dresses.'[265] Anne's diary is her first priority. Diaries preserve memories; they archive lives. Above clothes and accessories, Anne's diary becomes the essential ally for her ordeal during those long months in hiding. Yet its body is fragile, paper-thin. How will it survive? she wonders.

At the point of her arrest in August 1944, Anne's diary as we now know it was still a loose and incoherent body – fragile in its state of incompletion. To the Nazi sergeant, Silberbauer, who burst through the attic door of the secret annexe where Anne and her family were living, it was nothing more than a miscellaneous assortment of papers: a black notebook, a school exercise book, a red and white checked autograph album, and several loose leaves of paper he tossed from a briefcase as he searched for supplies of money. Silberbauer would never have noticed Anne's terror at the thought of her diary being destroyed. But it is precisely because he paid so little attention to Anne's scattered sheets that her diary survived and was gathered and put into a drawer by Miep Gies, one of the secretaries working in the warehouse building beneath the annexe. Miep is really the heroine of Anne's narrative: it is Miep who supplied Anne with writing materials, and it is Miep who gathered up, along with another Frank family helper, Elisabeth 'Bep' Voskuijl, the scattered parts of this fragile body and stored it away in her desk drawer.

Unlike Anne, her diary is a survivor; it has an afterlife. In his Foreword to the Definitive Edition, the edition read all over the world, Otto Frank, Anne's father, reminds us that Anne wanted to be a published writer; she wanted her diary to be read.[266] Anne's diary is now an international monument, reminding all who read it of the history of Jewish persecution in Holland. But to Otto Frank, the diary's executor, the decision to publish the diary was surely more personal: a wish to exhume from the tragedy of his daughter's death the printed body she had always wished for. Surely in his decision to publish Anne's diary, Otto Frank responded according to the overwhelming measure of devotion to this idea he heard pouring from the pages of Anne's most precious possession: 'I hope I will be able to confide everything to you, as I have never been able to confide in anyone, and I hope you will be a great source of comfort and support.'[267] Here is Anne's journal religion, an unwavering belief in the intercessory power of the diary as counsellor, friend and creed. It is a moment of supplication but also of creation. Read posthumously, Anne's statement sounds like an uncanny prophecy on the diary's afterlife: her diary has brought comfort and support to millions of readers. Her diary is still read all over the world.

*

Four years before fifteen-year-old Anne was looking with dread at the contents of her diary scattered across the annexe floor, fifty-eight-year-old Virginia Woolf is scrabbling around her London house in search of lived remnants. It is October 22nd 1940 and both her London houses have been bombed. Tavistock Square is now only 'bricks & wood splinters'. Among the powdery ruins, she begins to forage for her diaries.[268] The day begins desperately. By the end of it, Woolf is crooning over the success of her rescue operation: '24 vols of diary saved', a 'great mass for [her] memoirs'.[269]

Woolf's diary entry that day is as muddled and fragmentary as the contents of her former home: a bric-a-brac heap of mentioned 'things', an anxious foraging for possessions. Cutting through all this muddle is the instinctive response: 'I began to hunt out my diaries', a phrase that comes in the middle of – 'A wind blowing through' and then the desperate and scrappy question, 'What cd we salvage?'[270] Woolf's three-part sentence is a desperate and primitive response to over-whelming loss; in the face of an essential structural disintegration, her house, and, with it, her domestic life, she responds with a survivor's instinct. Before too much time passes, she must snatch back her diaries from the face of death and destruction. Her diaries are the only way back to the domestic life set down over twenty-five years. It is a diarist's basic instinct.

Elegy

Like life, diaries are hard to give up. They become a habit. By the close of 1940, Woolf is reassessing her writing method, as she is her life. She begins to reminisce. Images of her childhood, her mother and father, appear like spectral forms.[271] By February 1940 she is mourning the 'lost thoughts' of her mental life, those that come to her at breakfast, or when she is 'up to [her] knees in mud', on Asheham Down, or walking along the river bank.[272] The war has created an intense, extended present tense, but she is not using the time and space well.

To write like a naturalist, she decides, might suit her better. But Woolf has always written like a naturalist. In her mind's eye the world is filled with a myriad of species whose identities need pinning down. Woolf is a spotter of human species within their natural habitats. We need only think of Mrs Ramsay in Woolf's elegiac novel *To the Lighthouse* to understand that Woolf is a creator of aesthetic consciousness. She is interested in how people, by means of their inner life, turn other people and things into objects worth looking at, subjects worth seeing. Woolf writes in order to capture the precise movements and effect of Mrs Ramsay crossing a room, Mrs Ramsay at her dressing table with her children, playing with her pearls. Woolf's diary is much like Mrs Ramsay 'winding' life around her into a ball. From this tightly wound ball of wool comes a 'little book', a series of 'little books'.[273] Posterity.

By the end of her life, Woolf has nearly 30 such books all sitting on the shelf of her room. Her diary, she senses, is yet another work of unfinished fiction: rough, unedited, overly verbose. Now, at the end of her life, she is nervous about what she might find there.[274] In the final count, will she have let herself down? In a plain but painfully tender suicide note she leaves for Leonard, she asks him to 'destroy all my papers'.[275] It is a rash request. Sensibly, he never complies.

Diary-Memoir

Woolf's diary begins and ends its life with thoughts of the sea. One month after beginning her first diary she is dragged to Bognor on a miserable winter sojourn. Her diary, in the guise of Miss Jan, goes with her. Bognor, she complains, is 'muddy misty flat utterly stupid'. As she will say of Brighton a few months later, it is a 'disgraceful place'.[276] Miss Jan is beginning to sound like my mother, as indeed Miss Jan sounds like a version of Virginia Stephen's mother, Julia.

'Disgraceful' was a word my mother used a lot. Her children were frequently 'disgraceful'. To be disgraceful was to muddy all our nice white clothes, the clothes she had lovingly made for us, the clothes that nearly turned her blind. In my case that was an unbearably heavy white crochet dress that sat on me like ten dead Victorian aunties. You couldn't do anything in it. You certainly couldn't have brothers.

*

We spent a lot of our childhood bicycling around on 'old bangers' as we called our dilapidated bicycles. None of them passed the school cycling proficiency test. On test days we always had to borrow other people's bikes. Despite all the mud and drizzle coming off the country lanes around our seaside town, the murky footpath over to the West Beach, my mother insisted I wore white. White was pristine and proper. White was Victorian and nice.

When my mother sent us outdoors on our bikes she had no idea that we were going over to West Sands to try to find the nudists. 'Perverts' my aunt said. 'Disgraceful. You stay away.' When I read of young Woolf bicycling around Bognor I'm reminded of our trips towards West Sands. Teenage Virginia goes bicycling with her brothers and sisters and Miss Jan and the episode quickly turns into a high-spirited tantrum. Miss Jan is a mood and a landscape, she is an extension of the bad weather (which in January is disgraceful), she is pure feeling, she is a cross girl-lady on a bicycle. Miss Jan is the young diarist finding momentum, a subject and a voice.

'The mist blew in our faces, the mud spirted all over us – and behold – here was a school of little boys marching towards us! Their remarks shall not be entered here, Miss Jan says; we pushed on as fast as possible . . .'[277]

I love these lines because they sound so cross. Only her diary will allow Virginia Stephen to be this cross. But being cross is part of finding her voice. To be cross like this is to know precisely what it is you would prefer to be doing while you waste your time doing something else. In the case of young Virginia this was to be tucked up in an armchair reading her Pepys.

Bognor is disgraceful because Bognor brings on a bad temper. My mother associated Bognor with a glum mood. She knew there was nothing more desolate than a seaside town in winter. A soggy pier and a puddle-filled front really was the end. For that reason and many others – my mother's snobbish horror at the thought of a Butlins holiday being one – we were never sent to Bognor. The very mention of Bognor made her turn pale and cross. When the invitations from school friends came in they were promptly thrown in the rubbish. For that reason, I always think of Bognor as lying next to the sea in a plastic bin.

*

By the end of 1897 Miss Jan has disappeared, but the sea stays on. In her final entry, written on Monday, March 24th 1941, Woolf records a 'curious sea side feeling in the air'. She is back inside her seaside town, her dilapidated mood.

Leonard has brought her to Brighton to meet a doctor friend, Octavia Wilberforce. There is courage in that name, a will to go on. But blankets of cloud and sea hover around the edge. Octavia Wilberforce disappears behind clouds and Virginia Woolf, aged fifty-nine, finds herself stranded and alone at the end of the pier. She writes:

> A curious sea side feeling in the air today. It reminds me of lodgings on a parade at Easter. Everyone leaning against the wind, nipped & silenced. All pulp removed. This windy corner.[278]

Behind these lines I can see fifteen-year-old Virginia Stephen bicycling out of Bognor. I read back to that early entry: 'Another week of drizzle in that muddy misty flat utterly stupid Bognor (the name suits it) would have driven me to the end of the pier and into the dirty yellow sea beneath – (Hear hear)' Between these two versions, one more splintered than the other, I find a complete sentence; a continuous self, Virginia Woolf both young and old: 'It would have driven me to the end of the pier and into the dirty yellow sea beneath . . .' That is to say, 'This windy corner would have driven me to the end of the pier and into the dirty yellow sea beneath – (Hear hear). This windy corner where everyone leans against the wind.'[279]

Beneath these lines other forms arise, other seaside towns. Mine. Littlehampton, West Sussex, four miles along the coast from Bognor, 15 miles west of Brighton.

My grandmother leaning against the wind as she turns the corner from the seafront, between Granville Road and Norfolk Gardens, named after the Duke of Norfolk. Norfolk Gardens, where all the alcoholics and drug addicts live. Granville Road, where we live, in a house rented out by the council, a house whose hallway was stuffed with dirty bicycles.

My grandmother, whose flat was on Norfolk Terrace, just off the front, round the corner. The silence in the stairwell as she crawled up on all fours at the end of her life, with all her pulp removed.

My grandmother's feet turned upwards towards me, brown with tights. Silence in the thick blue carpet as I followed behind with the shopping. As I lifted the dirty mugs from the sink and washed them out to save her hands, all nipped in.

My grandmother's flat where I first learned to touch-type aged eight, before sharing porridge.

My grandmother who arrived every morning at eight with a basket full of eight pints of milk and three loaves of bread at least to break the silence of our house.

My grandmother, who loved Christmas oranges and taught me how to peel them carefully with a knife.

My grandmother who always knew what colour and how clean the sea was.

My grandmother who spent most of her life with her hands in the dirty yellow sea, our dishwater.

My grandmother, turning the windy corner on her bike, laden with milk and bread.

My grandmother, looking back, and waving. Waving and wobbling.

'Disgraceful,' my mother said, 'to bike like that, in this wind. With hands like that. Disgraceful, Sally. Don't you ever do that. Not on this windy corner. Not if you want to go on living, young lady!'

WHY AND HOW TO
KEEP A DIARY

Cassandra Mortmain would tell you that the reason you should keep a diary is to practise writing your novel: that and your speed-writing. Diary writing is good for your style. In your diary you can capture conversation; become more erudite and interesting. Cassandra Mortmain will tell you that anyone who wishes to write ought to keep a diary, or a journal as she prefers to call it.

I would tell you that diary writing is for anyone who wants a small enclave for reflection or creative thinking beyond the endless List of Things to Do (although these can also be tucked away in a diary and either forgotten about or more usefully contained). If this is so then you might want to carve out some diary space and time. My attempts at diary writing haven't been as determined as young Cassandra's. But at crucial moments in my life my diary has kept me intact. If nothing else, it has been a demonstration of privacy when privacy and selfhood were both thin on the ground. Even as a child my diary was a place of refuge from an overly managed and interfering world.

As an adult, my diary allows me to cling on to some sense of a continuous identity: a self that reflects and observes, a self that takes time out from the war on email and phone calls and the relentless round of marking; all the daily disturbances and distractions that poke holes in my brain. Keeping a diary can also afford you some slow-time. Here, you might make better decisions. As Cassandra Mortmain tells herself, her diary is somewhere she can try to make words flow. Your diary might be a place to rehearse those difficult speeches with those difficult people: our friends, colleagues and relations. As President John Adams knew, a diary can help produce eloquence.

Diary-keeping is a mild to moderate religion. It needs temporal commitment, some degree of organisation. I would advise anyone to keep a diary if they need some creative or reflective hook in their life; somewhere you can hang on to the parts of you that get lost in chores, the school run, the round of marking, the administrative morass of emails, guilty thoughts about not hoovering and then hoovering. I'd recommend something small: a compact notepad or notebook if you prefer paper. Keep your diary close to your person, in your bag or laptop bag; or, if your diary is to be a home-bound creature, keep it under your bed or in your bedside drawer. Don't let it stray too far from you in case of fire (think Pepys) or, here in Oxford, floods. And then there are the more personal hazards of keeping a diary: those nosey friends and relations, those lovers, those diary snoops.

I find that my diary becomes overwhelmingly useful when I turn to it as a sanctuary from shame: 'shame', from the Proto-Indo-European word, 'skem', meaning to cover. A diary can offer good cover from embarrassment and humiliation. So it was for Pepys with his medley of naughty dalliances. His diary code kept him well hidden, although not from his own private blushes. That is where diaries become really useful. They allow us a space in which to tramp around our secret terrain of shame. In my journal I keep notes on healthful habits I sincerely hope to develop: fast days (that never happen); shopping lists; a list of books I will read this summer; emails I must write; new people I should connect with; art shows I'd like to see; films I must catch up on; my internal hoard of should-dos and oughts, the experiences I believe will, in the mode of Boswell's journal, improve my character.

How To Keep a Diary Like ...

Sylvia Plath

Find yourself a good view. Sit by a window, somewhere with a vista. You'll want to see trees and sky, gain some perspective. Seventeen-year-old Plath sat at the top of her house in Wellesley, Massachusetts. It made her feel grander, larger. She loved the stars, the sky, trees; her late poems are full of these. Map yourself in relation to nature. Make yourself part of a natural setting. It is comforting to know where you are before you begin, to practise observing the sights around you. Sylvia Plath was happy knowing she was part of a natural scheme of things. Windows offer a frame for thinking through. A view from a window contains a limited number of subjects. A scene from a window is a ready-made composition. You already have something to write about, something larger than yourself, perhaps more interesting.

Sylvia Plath also liked to type up her journals. My grandmother taught me how to touch-type. I can type faster than I can write by hand, and I type as I think. Plath typed up her journal entries – the famous 'Girl who would be God' passage – because it made her feel more professional. There must have been something quite resolute and ultimate about the sound of a fifties typewriter clackety-clacking away. Nowadays we can delete anything we type on to our blank screen, but I've also acquired the habit of keeping a diary on my iPhone, in the 'Notes' section. I like the simulation of lined notepads. They remind me of being at school, and then the comforting yellow margin at the top. The aesthetic is juvenile and relaxing. Each time I open up my 'Notes' folder on my phone I'm surprised to see how much I've filed away there, tippety-tap. I like the experience of rediscovering those notes some days or weeks later, when those thoughts have completely disappeared from view. It is reassuring to discover that you have an archive of thoughts. You are not just a complete blank. Practise storing away words, phrases, favourite lines from novels or poetry or film. Turn your iPhone into a commonplace book. Create something to look back over, a horizon of thought.

Like Virginia Woolf

Begin by making your own diary-books. Find some old books in a second-hand shop or a car boot sale, books with good covers and bindings. Pull out some pages and fill them with your own choice of paper. Disguise your diary inside old school textbooks, the ones that used to teach grammar. Virginia Woolf was appalled by her negligent grammar. But grammar was not the point. Practise writing with and without it. Allow yourself to move. Woolf galloped through sentences in her diary, in a haphazard way. 'It loosens the ligaments,' she said. Her diary was somewhere she could appear 'slovenly' and 'elastic'. Not everything we jot down in our diaries needs to be carefully thought out. Put on baggy clothes. Relax your mental joints. No one but you is looking. Let your brain go loose and floppy. Let your hand lead the way. Get inside your body and find a rhythm. Bring your brain into contact with your breathing. Let go.

Find a comfy chair. Woolf liked to sit in an armchair. Settle into the back of a good chair. Plant your feet firmly on the floor. Choose a time that feels a little in between here and there, between tea and dinner, perhaps at twilight in the winter. Your imagination may run more freely then, as the light is fading. You'll forget the obligations of the day. Woolf often wrote between four and six in the afternoon. Light is crucial when you are writing. Think about the quality of light you prefer. Light sets the mood and for Woolf the hours between four and six held a certain uncanny atmosphere.

Admittedly she didn't have children or many family responsibilities. Carve out a space between mealtimes, or around nap times. Disappear for twenty minutes or so and don't tell anyone in your household where you are going. Sit outside in the garden shed, or turn the lock on the bathroom door. Don't explain yourself to anyone but your diary for a while.

Like Samuel Pepys

Find yourself a closet, somewhere you can store yourself away. Small spaces can bring focus. Pepys fretted about keeping his closet clean, especially after the Great Fire. There is a lot to be said for having a space to write and think in that is clean and tidy. Pepys often wrote his 'journall' in the closet of his office, other times in his chamber at home. 'And I to my closet in my office, to perfect my Journall, and to read my solemne vows and so to bed.'

Pepys made promises to himself in his journal. He kept good order. His method was exacting. He chose a calf-bound book filled with pages marked out by red ruled lines around the upper and outer margins. In the seventeenth century these sorts of books were typically used as commonplace books, places to store away lists of words or phrases, snatches of thought, interesting quotations, bits of philosophy. Alongside his diary he kept a 'by-book' for notes and memoranda that he often copied into his diary. Pepys was a fussy diary-keeper, but there is something to be said for his neatness. Like a good Puritan, he associated journal writing with vows. A journal is a good place to keep a set of promises to yourself. It might be painful to read them when you've broken them, but you can at least track the measure of your will.

Choose a large A5 hardbound notebook, one filled with ruled lines, and draw up a table of key words or prompts to reflect upon. Collect lines of poetry or song lyrics that provoke thinking. Writing out lines of poetry is one way to calm your mind.

Keep a list of things to do on one side of the page but then respond with a set of practical solutions on the other side.

Draw up lined tables to contain your goals. The discipline of creating a table is a reassuring one. Write in shorthand. Tasks seem simpler when they are written in brief. You don't need to know Pepys's Shelton code, but you could practise developing a list of symbols of your own, or a colour code. Perhaps that way you can convince yourself that everything you swear to do will be good for you. Practise a healthy bit of self-deceit. Dare yourself to do something brazen and new. You needn't buy a wig but perhaps you can promise yourself a holiday, and then plan it in your journal. Pepys promised his wife things – portraits, clothes – as a way of improving relations. Why not promise yourself things you haven't yet dared to do to improve your own self-regard? That hot-air balloon ride you always wanted to take; that trip to Mount Fuji; singing lessons; a very expensive pair of blue handmade shoes. Use your journal as a way of storing up wishes, practical or otherwise.

Like James Boswell

Keeping a journal might make you a better person. According to James Boswell, his journal would improve his character. The staple of a good character was diverting conversation, so Boswell collected dialogue in his London Journal, and rehearsed speeches.

Buy yourself a small but sturdy writing bureau, as Boswell did when he moved into his Downing Street lodgings. Choose an elegant piece of furniture, something wooden with several drawers. The more drawers you have the more diaries you can store. You might want to keep two or three diaries for different purposes: one for recording conversation, another for reflecting upon the political situation: what to think about Jeremy Corbyn. My colleague's son does this and he hopes, at least, to be an MP.

Store up lots of paper. You might want to keep a drawer of spare paper, of all shapes and sizes and textures. Boswell got his writing supplies for free, from his landlord. When I worked at one Oxford college I took great delight in pillaging the stationery cupboard as a way of making up for my degradingly low salary. I used that paper to compose drafts.

Make sure your writing bureau has locks and keys. If you share a house you don't want anyone peeping. Boswell wrote with a lit fire and sometimes with his feet in 'milk-warm water'. Why not write your journal with your feet in a basin of warm water scented with oils? That way you will relate journaling to relaxation. Open up the door between your bureau-space and your bedroom so that you have a space to walk to and fro. Boswell ordered a door to be 'struck out' between his dining room and bedroom. Give yourself plenty of room to pace up and down.

Then, when you get tired of your domestic space, go out into the public sphere. Find a cosy coffee shop where the staff don't mind you lingering for some time, or talking to yourself. I have one friend who always sits and writes in coffee shops mouthing his words to himself out loud. I've caught him at it and I'm reminded of a parliamentarian practising his speech before he goes out to face his antagonists. James Boswell practised dialogue lifted from his journal in coffee shops. Writing and speaking are close cousins. Good writing should sound like someone speaking. Certainly, this is how Boswell learned to write. His journal was a public arena: he invited in his friends and acquaintances, his public as well as his private sphere. A journal is a dialogue with yourself. It might help you to

practise writing formal dialogue. Create an alternative character, a Dr Johnson, to whom you can address your cares and
concerns, to whom you can speak. Use the snatches of conversations you hear outside, in coffee shops and restaurants. Store
them away in your journal and turn them into something
more extended and elaborate. Who knows, a play might
emerge from this; a skit; a Broadway show.

Like Cassandra Mortmain

Choose an outlandish position. Perhaps a bath or a sink.
Wear something romantic and slightly shabby, definitely
something with holes in it. Light some candles (rose-scented
or lavender), and have some Shakespeare close by for refer-
ence. I recommend the comedies because things work out best
there.

Let your diary be the place where you fret over your
relationships, with your family, with your friends. Work out
here, in your diary, what sort of boyfriend or girlfriend you
want. Create your ideal beloved. You might want to turn to
Shakespeare for this. Beatrice eventually chose Benedict for
his humour and wit. He reminded her of herself. But that
might not always work. They had arguments, they liked to
spar. Try to work out what sort of person you'd like to spend
the rest of your life with. Make a list of the qualities you most
prefer. What comes first? Collect some literary quotations for
future dates. Practise learning them off by heart. Make a list of
literary characters. Who fares the best in Shakespeare; whose
marriage is most likely to last?

Write up your ideal future scenario and then your worst

case scenario. Try to imagine your future self. What will they be doing? What sort of person will they be living with? What sort of conversations will they be having? When you run out of words start to doodle. Doodle your tumble-down house in the country, your handsome gentleman farmer, your pasture of good-looking cows.

Daydream. Alternative lives (imagined) can be a useful way of reflecting upon the present: you in the here and now. Allow yourself to scribble around the edges of your current life. Soften the edges of what you see of yourself. Cross it out and start again.

NOTES

Introduction: My first Diary

1. Jeff Kinney, *Diary of a Wimpy Kid: A Novel in Cartoons* (London: Penguin, 2007), p.1.
2. To avoid confusion, I refer to 'Virginia Woolf' throughout, though, of course, before her marriage in 1912 to Leonard Woolf she was Virginia Stephen.
3. Virginia Woolf, *A Passionate Apprenticeship: The Early Journals*, ed. Mitchell A. Leaska (London: Hogarth Press, 1992), p.31.
4. *Passionate Apprentice*, p.15.
5. Samuel Pepys, *The Shorter Pepys* (London: Penguin Classics, 1993), p.66.
6. Ibid., p.66.
7. Ibid., p.69.
8. Ibid., p.61–2.
9. Philip Lejeune, *On Diary* (Honolulu: University of Hawaii Press, 2009), p.57.
10. *The Shorter Pepys*. 'Preface', p.xxxii.
11. Claire Tomalin, *Samuel Pepys: The Unequalled Self* (London: Penguin, 2003), p.80.
12. See Alexandra Johnson's 'Introduction' to her *A Brief History of Diaries* (London: Hesperus Press, 2011) for the emergence of the diary in fourteenth-century Italy, the gradual shift from a record of public life, the marketplace, to the private life of individuals such as Lapo Niccolini.

13. Lejeune, *On Diary*, p.61.
14. Molly McCarthy, 'Redeeming the Almanac', www.common-place.org, vol. 11, no. 1, October 2010.
15. Virginia Woolf, *The Diary of Virginia Woolf*, ed. Anne Olivier Bell, assisted by Andrew McNeillie, 5 vols. (London: Hogarth Press, 1979–1985), vol. I, p.266.
16. *Aspern*, no. 7, item 8, http://www.ubu.com/aspen/aspen7/diary.html
17. A term first coined by Ericsson in 1997 with the release of their GS88 phone.
18. 'The History of the Smart Phone', http://thenextweb.com/mobile/2011/12/06/the-history-of-the-smartphone/ accessed 02/02/2015.
19. 'Digital Journalling Methods', Julie Strietelmeier, February 20th, 2012. http://the-gadgeteer.com/2012/02/20/digital-journaling-methods accessed 02/02/2015.
20. *The Shorter Pepys*, p.220.
21. *The Diary of Virginia Woolf*, vol. I, pp.42–3.
22. Virginia Woolf, 'Papers on Pepys', *Books and Portraits: Some Further Selections from the Literary and Biographical Writings of Virginia Woolf*, ed. Mary Lyon (New York: Harcourt Brace Jovanovich, 1977)

Chapter One: Teenage Confessions

23. Susan Sontag, *Reborn: Early Diaries* (1947–1964), ed. David Reiff (London: Hamish Hamilton, 2008), pp.164–5.
24. www.oed.com, 'selfnesse', accessed 10/12/2014.
25. *Reborn*, p.165.
26. Ibid., p.165.
27. Sue Townsend, *The Secret Diary of Adrian Mole Aged 13 ¾* (London: Penguin, 2012), p.12.
28. St Augustine, The Confessions of Saint Augustine (Minneapolis: Filiquarian Publishing, 2008), p.56.
29. *The Confessions*, p.56.
30. A. A. Hodge, *A Short History of Creeds and Confessions* (1869), http://www.bibleresearcher.com/confessions.html
31. *Reborn*, p.166.
32. Gillian Flynn, *Gone Girl* (London: Weidenfeld & Nicolson, 2012) p.9.
33. *Reborn*, p.166.
34. *Eye Rhymes: Sylvia Plath's Art of the Visual*, ed. Kathleen Connors and Sally Bayley (Oxford: OUP, 2007), p.69.
35. Sylvia Plath, 'Lady Lazarus', *Ariel: The Restored Edition*, ed. Frieda Hughes (London: Faber & Faber, 2004), p.16.
36. *The Journals of Sylvia Plath: 1950–1962*, ed. Karen Kukil (London: Faber & Faber, 2000), p.99.
37. *The Journals of Sylvia Plath*, p.99.
38. Ibid., p.151.
39. *Eye Rhymes*, p.69.
40. Ralph Waldo Emerson, *Selected Journals 1820–1842*, ed. Lawrence Rosenwald (New York: Library of America, 2010), p.2.
41. Emerson, *Selected Journals*, p.2.

42. Ibid., p.91.
43. *The Journals of Sylvia Plath*, p.123.
44. Ibid., p.85.
45. Ibid., p.121.
46. Quoted in *Eye Rhymes*, p.69.
47. *Reborn*, p.166.
48. Quoted in *Eye Rhymes*, p.43.
49. *The Journals of Sylvia Plath*, p.9.
50. Quoted in *The Journals of Sylvia Plath*, p.7.

Chapter Two: Diary Dawdling

51. *The Diary of Virginia Woolf*, p.266.
52. *Passionate Apprentice*, pp.177–8.
53. Ibid., pp.159–60.
54. *The Diary of Virginia Woolf*, vol. I, pp.39, 321.
55. Ibid., vol. I, p.49.
56. Ibid., vol. I, p.49.
57. Ibid., vol. I, p.49.
58. Ibid., vol. III, pp.3, 218.
59. Ibid., vol. I, p.291.
60. Ibid., vol. III, p.249.
61. *Boswell's London Journal 1762–1763*, ed. Frederick A. Pottle (London: The Reprint Society, 1952), p.39.
62. *London Journal*, p.49.
63. Peter Martin, *A Life of James Boswell* (London: Weidenfeld & Nicolson, 1999), p.134.
64. *Life of James Boswell*, pp.17, 114.
65. *London Journal*, p.50.
66. Ibid., p.49.
67. Ibid., p.59.
68. Ibid., p.183.
69. *Life of James Boswell*, p.134.
70. *London Journal*, p.320.
71. Ibid., pp.294–5.
72. Ibid., p.320.
73. Ibid., p.320.
74. *Life of James Boswell*, p.105.
75. *London Journal*, p.320.
76. Francis Bacon, 'Of Travel', in *Essays* (London: Everyman, 1994), p.54.

77. John Locke, *An Essay Concerning Human Understanding* (1689), ed. Pauline Phemister (Oxford: Oxford University Press, 2008).

78. Steven Johnson, *Where Good Ideas Come from: The Seven Patterns of Innovation* (London: Allen Lane, 2010).

79. Lucia Dacome, 'Noting the Mind: Commonplace Books and the Pursuit of the Self in Eighteenth Century Britain', *Journal of the History of Ideas*, vol. 65, no. 4 (October 2004), pp. 603–25.

80. Locke, *An Essay Concerning Human Understanding*.

81. *Life of James Boswell*, p. 155.

82. James Boswell, *Journal of a Tour to the Hebrides* (London: Penguin Books, 1984), pp. 185–6.

83. *Journal of a Tour to the Hebrides*, pp. 185–6.

84. *The Journals of Sylvia Plath*, pp. 547–8.

85. *Life of James Boswell*, p. 114.

86. *The Journals of Sylvia Plath*, pp. 554–68.

87. Ibid., p. 564.

88. Ibid., pp. 564–5.

89. Samuel Johnson, letter to Hester Thrale, September 21st 1773.

90. Quoted in Ari N. Schulman, *The New Atlantis*, http://www.vagablogging.net/rp/vagabonding-life/notes-from-the-collective-travel-mind.

91. See, for example, *The Journals of Sylvia Plath*, p. 269.

92. *The Diary of Virginia Woolf*, vol. III, p. 88.

93. Ibid., vol. IV, pp. 90–91.

Chapter Three: Back to Nature

94. *The Diary of Virginia Woolf,* vol. IV, p.100.
95. Ibid., vol. V, p.266.
96. Ibid., vol. III, pp.229, 254.
97. Ibid., vol. IV, p.110.
98. Ibid., vol. III, p.109.
99. Ibid., vol. I, p.148.
100. *Journals of Henry David Thoreau,* ed. Bradford Torrey and Francis H. Allen, 14 vols (Boston: Houghton Mifflin, 1949), vol. VII, p.371; vol. I, p.136.
101. Ibid., vol. I, p.136.
102. Ibid., vol. XII, pp.90–92.
103. Ibid., vol. IV, p.350.
104. *Kilvert's Diary, 1870–1879,* ed. William Plomer (London: Penguin, 1978), p.9.
105. *Kilvert's Diary,* pp.32–3.
106. Ibid., p.31.
107. Ibid., p.237.
108. Gerard Manley Hopkins, *Poems and Prose* (London: Penguin Classics, 1985), p.108.
109. *Poems and Prose,* p.108.
110. Mary Ellen Bellanca, 'Gerard Manley Hopkins' Journal and the Poetics of Natural History', *Nineteenth Century Prose,* September 22nd, 1998, p.2.
111. *Poems and Prose,* p.121.
112. Ibid., pp.110, 114, 121.
113. Ibid., p.121.
114. George Orwell, *Diaries* (London: Penguin, 2010), p.75.
115. Orwell, *Diaries,* p.77.
116. Ibid., p.208.

117. Ibid., p. 206.
118. Ibid., p. 157.

Chapter Four: Going Public

119. *The Unequalled Self*, p.221.
120. Benjamin Kohlmann, 'Men of Sobriety and Business: Pepys, Privacy and Public Duty', *Review of English Studies*, New Series, vol. 61, no. 251 (2009), p.561.
121. *The Unequalled Self*, p.127.
122. *The Shorter Pepys*, p.130.
123. Ibid., p.130.
124. J. Habermas, *The Structural Transformation of the Public Sphere*, trans. T. Burger with F. Lawrence (Cambridge: Polity Press, 1989)..
125. Steve Pincus, 'Coffee Politicians Does Create: Coffeehouses and Restoration Political Culture', *Journal of Modern History*, vol. 67, no. 4 (December 1995), p.819.
126. *Structural Transformation of the Public Sphere*, p.20.
127. Michael McKeon, *The Secret History of Domesticity: Public, Private, and the Division of Knowledge* (Baltimore: Johns Hopkins University Press, 2005), pp.126–7.
128. *Structural Transformation of the Public Sphere*, p.xi.
129. *The Shorter Pepys*, p.195.
130. Ibid., pp.193–5.
131. Ibid., pp.708–9.
132. Ibid., p.1010.
133. Ibid., p.1009.
134. Ibid., p.1011.
135. Ibid., p.1005.
136. 'Introduction', *The Diary of Samuel Pepys*, ed. R.C. Latham and W. Matthews, vol. I (1660) (London: Harper Collins, 1995), p.xxviii.
137. Ryan Holston, 'Burke's Historical Morality', *Humanitas*, vol.

XX, nos.1 and 2, 2007, p.41. Burke argues his point on historical consciousness in *Reflections on the French Revolution in France* (1790).

138. *The Diary of John Adams*, Diary 1, March 15th, 1756, *Adams Family Papers: An Electronic Archive*, Massachusetts Historical Society. http://www.masshist.org/digitaladams/

139. See, for example, David McCullough, *John Adams* (London: Simon & Schuster, 2001).

140. *The Diary of John Adams*, Diary 2, Spring 1759.

141. Frederick A. Pottle, 'Introduction', *Boswell's London Journal*, p.25.

142. *The Diary of John Adams*, Diary 2, Spring 1759.

143. Ibid., Diary 2, Spring 1759.

Chapter Five: In the Political Eye

144. *The Diary of John Adams*, Diary 38, December 6th 1782.
145. *The Shorter Pepys*, p.971.
146. Ibid., p.861.
147. Ibid., p.1015.
148. Ibid., p.591.
149. Alan Clark, Preface to *Diaries: In Power 1983–1992* (London: Weidenfeld & Nicolson, 2003).
150. *Diaries: In Power*, pp.143–4.
151. Ibid., p.131.
152. Alan Clark, *Diaries: Into Politics*, ed. Ion Trewin (London: Weidenfeld & Nicolson, 2000), p.3.
153. Ibid., p.5.
154. Ibid., p.5.
155. Ion Trewin, 'Forget the Sword of Truth, Wield Your Pen', http://www.independent.co.uk/opinion/commentators/ion-trewin-forget-the-sword-of-truth-wield-your-pen-629168.html
156. Tony Benn, *The Benn Diaries*, ed. Ruth Winstone (London: Arrow Books, 1996), p.51.
157. *The Benn Diaries*, p.26.
158. Chris Mullin in interview with Tom Dannet, 'On Political Diaries' in *Browser*, November 10th 2009, http://thebrowser.com/interviews/chris-mullin-on-political-diaries?page=2
159. *The Benn Diaries*, p.51.
160. Ibid., p.26.
161. *Diaries: In Power*, p.8.
162. Ibid., p.9.
163. Ibid., p.9.
164. Alan Clark, *The Last Diaries: In and Out of the Wilderness*,

1993–1999 (London: Weidenfeld & Nicholson, , 2003). p.147.

165. Ibid., p.144.

166. *The Benn Diaries*, p.37.

167. Ibid., p.37.

168. *The Shorter Pepys*, p.51.

169. *The Benn Diaries*, pp.312–13.

170. Ibid., p.309.

171. *The Diary of John Adams*, Diary 42.

172. *The Benn Diaries*, p.109.

173. *Diaries: In Power*, pp.249–50.

174. *Diary of John Adam*, Diary 26, Notes on Continental Congress, 16 February–April 1776.

175. Ibid., Diary 26.

176. *Diaries: In Power*, p.321.

177. *Diaries: Into Politics*, p.345.

178. Ibid., p.351.

179. Ibid., p.341.

180. Ibid., p.362.

181. Ibid., p.364.

182. Ibid., p.366.

183. Ibid., p.367.

Chapter Six: War and Disaster

184. *Diaries: Into Politics*, p.305.

185. Ibid., p.310.

186. *Off the Record: The Private Papers of Harry S. Truman*, ed. Robert Ferrell, http://www.doug-long.com/hst.htm.

187. http://www.doug-long.com/hst.htm.

188. *The Diary of Virginia Woolf*, vol. v, p.166.

189. Ibid., vol. V, pp.232–3.

190. Ibid., vol V. pp.232–3.

191. *The Diaries of Evelyn Waugh*, ed. Michael Davie (London: Phoenix, 2009), p.462.

192. *The Diaries of Evelyn Waugh*, p.459.

193. Ibid., p.461.

194. Orwell, *Diaries*, pp.245–6.

195. *The Shorter Pepys*, pp.659–60.

196. Ibid., pp.662–3.

197. Ibid., p.661.

198. Ibid., p.661.

199. *The Diary of Virginia Woolf*, vol V, p.131.

200. Ibid., vol V, p.132.

201. *The Diaries of Evelyn Waugh*, p.457.

202. Ibid., p.464.

203. Ibid., p.473.

204. Ibid., p.554.

205. Virginia Woolf, *Mrs Dalloway*, ed. Elaine Showalter and Stella McNichol (London: Penguin, 2000).

206. Ibid., p.201.

207. *The Diaries of Evelyn Waugh*, p.558.

208. As Michael Davie notes, *The Diaries of Evelyn Waugh*, p.479.

209. *The Diaries of Evelyn Waugh*, p.502.

210. Ibid., p.503.
211. Ibid., p.514.
212. *The Shorter Pepys*, p.659.
213. Ibid., p.660.
214. Ibid., p.661.

Chapter Seven: Scandal

215. *The Shorter Pepys*, p. 520.

216. *The Diary of Samuel Pepys*, p. 574.

217. *The Shorter Pepys*, p. 697.

218. Ibid., p. 651.

219. Michael Davie, 'Preface', *The Diaries of Evelyn Waugh*, p. vii.

220. H. R. Haldeman, *The Haldeman Diaries: Inside the Nixon White House*, ed. Stephen E. Ambrose (New York: G. Putnam & Sons, 1994), p. 53.

221. *The Shorter Pepys*, p. 548.

222. Ibid., p. 989.

223. Ibid., p. 801.

224. Ibid., p. 798.

225. http://ranumspanat.com/html%20pages/Pepys.html.

226. *The Shorter Pepys*, p. 230.

227. Harry T. Baker, 'Early English Journalism', *Sewanee Review*, vol. 25, no. 4 (October 1917), p. 396

228. Robert Shephard, 'Court Factions in Early Modern England', *Journal of Modern History*, vol. 64, no. 4 (December 1992), pp. 721–45.

229. Barbara Benedict, *Curiosity: A Cultural History of Modern Inquiry* (Chicago: University of Chicago Press, 2001), p. 101.

230. *The Diary of Virginia Woolf*, vol. II, p. 177.

231. Ibid., vol. II, p. 177, ftn 1.

232. Ibid., vol. II, pp. 178–9.

233. *The Shorter Pepys*, p. 950.

234. Ibid., p. 953.

235. Ibid., p. 966.

236. Ibid., p. 967.

237. Ibid., p. 961.

238. Ibid., p.1023.
239. *The Journals of Mary Shelley 1814–1844*, ed. Paula R. Feldman and Diana Scott-Kilvert (Oxford: Oxford University Press, 1987) 2 vols., vol. I, p.6.
240. Ibid., p.7.
241. Ibid., p.7.
242. Fiona MacCarthy, *Byron: Life and Legend* (London: John Murray, 2002), pp.270–71.
243. *Byron: Life and Legend*, p.324.
244. Mary Shelley, *History of a Six Weeks' Tour* (London: T. Hookham, 1817), p.10.
245. Oscar Wilde, *De Profundis* (London: Methuen, 1905), p.23.
246. Appendix 2: Robert Ross's Preface to the 1905 British Edition of *De Profundis* in *The Complete Works of Oscar Wilde*, ed. Russell Jackson and Ian Small (Oxford: Oxford University Press, 2005), p.311.
247. *Oscar Wilde*, ed. Karl Beckson (Taylor & Francis, elibrary, 2005), p.19.
248. *Complete Works of Oscar Wilde*, p.159.
249. Appendix 2, *Complete Works of Oscar Wilde*, p.311.
250. http://twitter.com/#!/stephenfry/status/1174476459
251. http://www.famoustweeters.com/famous-ladygaga.htm
252. See Hannah Arendt, *The Human Condition* (Chicago: University of Chicago Press, 1958).
253. *The Unequalled Self*, p.359.
254. Ibid., p.360.
255. Ibid., pp.360–61.
256. *The Offensive Internet: Privacy, Speech and Reputation*, ed. Saul Levmore and Martha S. Nussbaum (Harvard: Harvard University Press, 2011), p.9.
257. Ibid., p.17.

258. Jonathan Franzen, *How to be Alone* (London: HarperCollins, 2010), p. 43.

259. *The Diary of Virginia Woolf*, vol. V, p. 276.

260. *The Penguin Book of Diaries*, ed. Ronald Blythe (London: Penguin, 1989), p. 17.

261. William Shakespeare, *Hamlet*, ed. Ann Thompson and Neil Taylor (London: Arden Shakespeare, 2006), V.ii. 354–363.

262. *The Diary of Virginia Woolf*, vol. V, p. 290.

263. Adam Nicolson, *The Smell of Summer Grass* (London: Harper Press, 2011), p. 113.

Conclusion: The Diary Afterlife

264. Doreen Roberts, 'Introduction', to Daniel Defoe, *Robinson Crusoe* (London: Wordsworth Classics, 2000), p.xiii.

265. Anne Frank, *The Diary of a Young Girl, The Definitive Edition*, ed. Otto H. Frank and Mirjam Pressler (London: Penguin, 2007), p.20.

266. 'Foreword', *Diary of a Young Girl*, p.v.

267. *Diary of a Young Girl*, p.1.

268. *The Diary of Virginia Woolf*, vol. V, p.331.

269. Ibid., vol. V, p.332.

270. Ibid., vol. V, p.331.

271. Ibid., vol. V, p.281.

272. Ibid., vol. V, p.263.

273. Ibid., vol. V, p.339.

274. Ibid., vol. V. p.339.

275. *Letters of Virginia Woolf*, vol. 6, March 28th 1941, p.487; see Alex Zwerdling, 'Mastering the Memoir: Woolf and the Family Legacy', *Modernism/modernity*, vol. 10, no. 1, January 2003, pp.165–88.

278. *Passionate Apprentice*, p.71.

279. Ibid., p.33.

278. *The Diary of Virginia Woolf*, vol. V, p.359.

279. *Passionate Apprentice*, p.33.

ACKNOWLEDGEMENTS

This is a book about writing and the writing of it has involved shedding many skins. Many people have helped me. I want to thank Matthew Clayton and Phil Connor at Unbound for first reading the manuscript and seeing its potential. A very large thank you to Craig Adams, my editor, for seeing its best self and helping me tease that out. The book would be very different without you. Thank you for encouraging me to drop old habits and adopt new. Thank you for sharing your passion for innovative forms of writing and education. Thank you to Isobel Frankish for her kind and caring support as Managing Editor at Unbound and to Amy Winchester at Unbound for her enthusiasm for promoting the book. Thank you also to Georgia Odd and Emily Shipp for clever marketing schemes.

Many people have helped me by reading this book in its various guises. Thank you to Tom MacFaul, who first suggested I send my book to Unbound and for his fabulous help with devising a title. Thank you to April Pierce for her very careful and sensitive reading in the final stages; to Noreen Masud for her intellectual excitement, big brain and large, generous and inspirational presence in the world; to Tamsin Huxford for her careful suggestions; to John Warriner for his reading time and his enthusiasm; to Ben Morgan for being such a good writer and friend; to Becky Birrell for her devotion to thinking through Virginia Woolf. A big thank you to my talented friend and kindred spirit, Suzie Hanna, for sharing her magical film, 'The Girl Who Would Be God' about the young, creative life of Sylvia Plath. Thank you also to Lyndall Gordon, Charlie Lee Potter and to Jemima Hunt for their support as women and as writers and to Christine Gerrard for her friendship, wisdom and support of the eighteenth century tradition of subscription publishing.

A big thank you to Nick Morgan for his reading of the manuscript early on and for his infectious commitment to the intellectual imagination. Thank you to all who have encouraged me to write imaginatively and independently: Sophie Ratcliffe, Will May, Andrew Blades, Sunetra Gupta, Amit Chaudhuri, Dennis Harrison (whose bookshop, The Albion Beatnik on Walton Street, Oxford, we should all frequent), Steven Isenberg, Linda Gates, Una Eve, Thalia Suzuma, Tracy Brain, Sanders Bernstein, Angie Johnson, Alexis Kirschbaum, William Bedford, Amy Waite, John Hood, Kelsey Finkel, Nadia Hilliard, Blake Ewing, Nick Rawlins, Alexandra Lewis, Caroline Dixon-Ward, Elisabeth Gray and Margaret Scarborough for sharing her beautifully observed thoughts on journal writing. They are some of the best journal entries I have ever read. Margaret, you are a true journal-philosopher. Thank you to Mikaela Liotta for sharing her stunning book art and to Tania Rajabian for her tender painting, 'Sally's Diary'.

Thank you to all my generous subscribers, especially to Claire Hansen, Catherine Dru, Pamela Huxford, Philip Stewart, Ray Hilliard, Suzie Hanna, Celeste-Marie Bernier, Elisabeth Gray. I have been extraordinarily fortunate in being able to teach some brilliant young people with whom I have shared conversations about many of the writers in this book.

You are also part of this book: Noreen Masud, Nick Morgan, Jack Harris, Simon Thomas, Sinead Esler, Amy Waite, Becky Birrell, Sanders Bernstein, Grace Chesterton, Pascale Hughes, Rosie Fearon, Eve Jackson, Hattie Ghaui, Marrium Khan, April Peake, Tania Rajabian, Adam Crozier, Jennifer Cownie, Alice Nutting, Alice James, Gabriel Pinos, Kelsey Finkel, Julia Buxton, Mary Livingstone, Olivia Reilly, Jon Turner, Chiara Shea, Katy Edge, Emma Campbell Webster, Polly Findlay, James Gillard, Ryan Hocking, Ali Chetwynd, Alexandra Coghlan, Baldwin Li, Richard Stanton, Hugh Montgomery, Michelle Madsen, Claire Butterworth, Becca Marriot, Andrew Dagnell, Ceri Hughes, Matt Hill, Christy Edwall, Gerard Whyte, Ticci Randall, Alexander Heritage, Jonathan Lyon, Josefin Holmstrom, Lara Piegeler, Adeela Khan, Sophie Jamieson, Ella Cory-Wright, Thomas Hughes, Bridget Dru, Anna-Clare Mitchell, Maisie Lawrence, Skye Verbruggen, Katharina Dixon-Ward, Georgie Newson.

Thank you to my English teachers at Brighton Sixth Form College, Vicky Craven and Margaret Blythe, during those difficult years. And thank you to all my current students at Lady Margaret Hall who have all shown so much interest.

Thank you to my families for their continued support and for tolerating my habits, especially to my parents, Rosemary and Eric Thompson, my brothers Jamie, Daniel and Richard (my very first subscriber), my sister Susie, my sister-in-law, Karen and my inspirational writing sister, Catalina Gaya who also loves narrative. Thank you to my nephew Joe for sacrificing some of his pocket money for this book. Thank you to Nasir for everything that you have given and still give me.

Finally, thank you to my grandmother, Maisie, for teaching me to type when I was eight and to my grandmother, Grace Ottmann, for loving the sound of words so much.

SUBSCRIBERS

Unbound is a new kind of publishing house. Our books are funded directly by readers. This was a very popular idea during the late eighteenth and early nineteenth centuries. Now we have revived it for the internet age. It allows authors to write the books they really want to write and readers to support the writing they would most like to see published.

The names listed below are of readers who have pledged their support and made this book happen. If you'd like to join them, visit: www.unbound.co.uk.

Jacob Adelman
Manoela Afonso
Seun Alabi
Nicholas Allan
Patrick Andelic
Penny Arrowood
Liz Atkinson
James Aylett
Ann Ballinger
Jason Ballinger
John Baranik
Laura Barnicoat

Heather Barr
Helen Barr
Jenny Barrett
Chris Barron
Zosh Barton
Dan Bayley
Ethan Bayley
Hayden Bayley
James Bayley
Jasper Bayley
Jensen Bayley
William Bedford

Eva Bednar
Daniel Benton
Celeste-Marie Bernier
Sanders Bernstein
Ekaterina Berova
Becky Birrell
Yvonne Blackburn
Andrew Blades
Nigel Blades
Val Borba
Nigel Bowles
Jeanette Boyd
Jo Bradshaw
Edward Bragg
Tracy Brain
Richard WH Bray
Beth Breeze
Eithne Brennan
Colin Brett
Liz & Roger Brett
Anne Broadbridge
Gemma Brooks
Claire Bruten
Debi Bryant
Ken Burt
Kate Bussert
Clare Butterworth
Julia Buxton
Andrew Campling
Josh Carpenter
Anna Carson-Parker
Maby Cat

Gérard Celli
Amit Chaudhuri
Grace Chesterton
Ravichandra Chittampalli
Charlie Clarke
Paul Clarke
Monika Class
Alexandra Coghlan
Patricia Colyer
Helen Compson
Philip Connor
Tom Cook
David Cooke
Olivia Cormack
Rachel Coward
Sylvia Coward
Jennifer Cownie
John Crawford
Sheryl Crown
Adam Crozier
Gaoziyan Cui
Matilda Curtis
Emma Cuthbert
Tom Cutterham
Katharina D-W
Emma D'Aniello
Trisha D'Hoker
Andrew Dagnell
Jane Dallaway
   (in memory of Zoe
   who kept a diary)
Michael Daniels

Heather Dansie

Huw David

Chris Davies

Harriet Davies

Matt & Owen Davies

Xon de Ros

Elizabeth Debski

Simon Dennis

Sushila Dhall

Dawn Dickinson

Catherine Dodsworth

Katya Dolgodvorova

Bridget Dru

Catherine Dru

Carrie Dunham-LaGree

Vivienne Dunstan

Elaine Dye

Claire Hansen Eaton

Christy Edwall

Jonathan Ellis

Sinéad Esler

Una Eve

Alexander Ewing

Chloe Fairbanks

Lafrance Family

Cameron Finlay

Anthea Finn

Paraic Finnerty

Marie Fitzpatrick

Kate Flatt

Paula J. Francisco

Hamish Fraser

Jonathan French

Tom Freston

Sonia Friel

Emily Frisella

Mark Gamble

Ines Garcia

Linda Gates

Catalina Gaya

Christine Gerrard

Harriet Ghaui

James Gillard

Jennie Gillions

Alexandra Glass

William Goldsmith

Elisabeth Gray

Mark Krishan Gray

Jane Griffiths

Sunetra Gupta

Lucy Gwynn

Ursula Hackett

Miranda Hall

Christine Hallett

Heather Hamill

Suzie Hanna

Susie Harries

Alexandra Harris

Jack Harris

Jennifer Harris

Dennis Harrison

Virginia Hartley

Dave Harvey

Lisa Hayter

David Hebblethwaite
Alexander Heritage
Lesley Heritage
Nick Hewlett
Mark Hildred
Mason Hill
Matt Rowland Hill
Nadia Hilliard
Ray Hilliard
Rachel Hirst
Martin Hitchcock
George Hoare
Ryan Hocking
James Edward Hodkinson
Pamela Hollenbeck
Samantha Holloway
Josefin Holmström
Jonathan Holt
John Hood
Jennifer Hoogewerf-McComb
Anthony Howcroft
Gill Howcroft
Matt Huggins
Ceri Hughes
Thomas Hughes
Jemima Hunt
Tamsin Huxford
Marie Irshad
Johari Ismail
Paula Izenstein
Bianca Jackson
Jennifer Jackson

Alice James
Felicity James
Paul James
Sophie Jamieson
Lyndsey Jenkins
Sophia Jennings
Marjorie Johns
Angie Johnson
Chris Johnson
Mark Jones
Sarah Jones
Katie Jowett
Caroline Joyce
Edward Kanterian
Stephanie Kelley
Aidan Kendrick
Richard Kerridge
Adeela Khan
Nasir Khan
Waseem Khan
Dan Kieran
Maree Kimberley
Nicola King
Kirsty Kitchen
Andrew Klevan
Shivani Kochhar
Naomi Kreitman
Marc Lafrance
Georgie Laming
Sally Lane
Nikki Lark-Spain
Maisie Lawrence

Henry C H Lee

Megan Lee

Tracy Lee-Newman

Charlie Lee-Potter

Alexandra Lewis

Bex Lewis

Elen Lewis

Karen Liebreich

Caroline Lien

Mikaela Liotta

Mary Livingstone

Jacob Lloyd

Benjamin Lomas

Sarah Longman

Paul Lorton Jr

HHB Ltd

Bevil Luck

Ella Luo

Andrea MacDonald

Roderick Macfaul

Tom MacFaul

Seonaid Mackenzie

Michelle Madsen

Philippa Manasseh

Liz Marchbank

Noreen Masud

Elizabeth May

Will May

Laura Mazzola

Frankie McCoy

Peter McDonald

Ashley McGovern

Joe McGuinness

Jamie McKendrick

Tegan McLeod

Chris Miller

Danny Mills

Ruth Mitchell

John Mitchinson

Michael Monoyios

Hugh Montgomery

Ben Morgan

Nick Morgan

Rose Morley

Thomas Moynihan

Jane Mulvagh

Olive Murray

Megan Murray-Pepper

Natasha Musto

Helen Nash

Carlo Navato

Lucy Newlyn

Jo Newson

Anabelle Nuelle

Jenni Nuttall

Alice Nutting

Johanna O'Connor

Sasha O'Connor

Andi Ottmann

Bruce Ottmann

Kathryn Ottmann

Tim Ottmann

Alaw Rhys Owen

Simon Palfrey

Nicole Panizza
Julia Parker
Luke Parks
April Peake
Nicholas Perkins
Sarah Pethybridge
Lydia Phillips
Caroline Phinney
Catherine Pickersgill
Pickles
Charles Pidgeon
Lara K Piegeler
April Pierce
Sophie Pitman
Katherine Pole
Justin Pollard
Katarina Polonsky
Jackie Potter
Alex Pryce
Alan Pymer
Andy & Cathy Pymer
Joe Quinlan
Ruth Quinlan
Susie Quinlan
Tania Rajabian
Helen Rampton
Victoria Randall
Helen Rappaport
Sophie Ratcliffe
John Rawlins
Jane Rawson
Matthew Redhead

Amber Regis
Clancy Reid
Fiona Reid
Olivia Reilly
Valerie Reilly
Josephine Reynell
Phyllis Richardson
Suzanne Robey
Joanna & Graeme Robinson
Chris Robson
David Roman
Robyn Roscoe
James Rowsell
Tessa Roynon
Igal Sarna
Jenna Sauber
M. Scarborough
Rory Scarfe
Lotta Schneidemesser
Jessica Schouela
Andrew Schuman
Becca Schwartz
Isabel Seligman
Catherine Shafto
Chiara Shea
Katy Shea
Mark Shepherd
Linda Shoare
Niamh Simpson
Eric Sinclair
Sujala Singh
Erin J. Slater

Douglas Smith

Emma Smith

Ruth Snary

Claire Snodgrass

Caryn Solomon

Joan Solomon

Katja Stein

Tiffany Stern

Joanne Steventon

Philip Stewart

Rachel Stirling

Aisling Stringer

Antony Strong

Libby Summers

Julie Sutherland

Thalia Suzuma

Adam Swift

Beverley Tarquini

Bridget Taylor

Maisie Taylor

Eric Thompson

Richard Thompson

Rosemary and Eric Thompson

Caroline Thomsen

Fred Titmouse

Margaret Tongue

Courtney Traub

Jon Turner

Marion Turner

Sally Turner

Paula Urwin

Mark Vent

Linda Verstraten

Amy W

Jo W

Toni Wallace

John Warriner

Pam & Dennis Wears

Andrew Weaver

Scott Weddell

Hannah Whelan

Isabelle Whitaker

Stuart White

Liam Whitton

Gerard Whyte

Amanda Wiggins

Ben Wilkinson-Turnbull

Mark Williams

Amy Winchester

Kieron Winn

Gretchen Woelfle

Danny Wolfson

Andreas Wolters

Alan Wright

Will Yeldham

Amy Yu

Jessica Yung

A NOTE ABOUT THE TYPE

'A Caslon-ridden country' was the description American typographer Bruce Rogers bestowed upon England as he sailed to its shores in 1916. Indeed, the popularity of Caslon – the typeface in which this book is set – had risen unabated since its revival in the 1840s. Originally designed around 1720 by a young gun engraver called William Caslon, the typeface became the embodiment of English typography, though its characteristics drew heavily upon the Dutch Fell types of Dirk Voskens and Christoffel van Dyck on which English printing had become dependent for some time. William Caslon reversed the flow of imported European types, beginning a type-founding dynasty that would span centuries.

Following the invention of machine typesetting in the late 1800s, the Monotype Corporation established itself near Redhill, Surrey. William Maxwell, one of the Corporation's first and biggest customers, was a Caslon man through and through: it was imperative for him to be able to set his preferred type mechanically. In carrying out his request in 1916, the Corporation mastered the technique of reproducing for the machine a heavily kerned type and one more regulated than was being cast in the United States. The Caslon design used in this book is by Carol Twombly, based on Caslon's own specimen pages printed in 1734.